Y0-BRY-227

Easy Microsoft® Excel 97

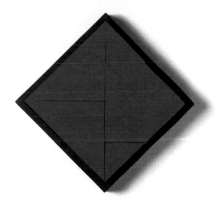

Elaine Marmel

que®

Easy Microsoft Excel 97

Copyright © 1997 Que® Corporation

All rights reserved. No part of this book shall be reproduced, stored in a retrieval system, or transmitted by any means, electronic, mechanical, photocopying, recording, or otherwise, without written permission from the publisher. No patent liability is assumed with respect to the use of the information contained herein. While every precaution has been taken in the preparation of this book, the publisher and author assume no responsibility for errors or omissions. Neither is any liability assumed for damages resulting from the use of the information contained herein. For information, address Que Corporation, 201 West 103rd Street, Indianapolis, IN 46290. You can reach Que's direct sales line by calling 1-800-428-5331.

Library of Congress Catalog Card Number: 96-71445

International Standard Book Number: 0-7897-1025-0

99 98   8 7 6 5 4 3 2

Interpretation of the printing code: the rightmost double-digit number is the year of the book's first printing; the rightmost single-digit number is the number of the book's printing. For example, a printing code of 97-1 shows that this copy of the book was printed during the first printing of the book in 1997.

Screen reproductions in this book were created by means of the program Collage Complete from Inner Media, Inc, Hollis, NH.

Printed in the United States of America

This book was produced digitally by Macmillan Computer Publishing and manufactured using computer-to-plate technology (a film-less process) by GAC/Shepard Poorman, Indianapolis, Indiana.

Credits

Publisher
Roland Elgey

Publishing Manager
Lynn E. Zingraf

Editorial Services Director
Elizabeth Keaffaber

Managing Editor
Michael Cunningham

Director of Marketing
Lynn E. Zingraf

Acquisitions Editor
Martha O'Sullivan

Technical Specialist
Nadeem Muhammed

Product Development Specialists
Melanie Palaisa
Nancy Warner

Technical Editor
Cynthia O'Brien

Production Editor
Audra Gable

Book Designers
Barbara Kordesh
Ruth Harvey

Cover Designers
Dan Armstrong
Kim Scott

Production Team
Tammy Ahrens
Toi Davis
Stephanie Hammett
Natalie Hollifield
Tom Missler
Angel Perez
Linda Quigley
Holly Wittenberg

Indexer
Cheryl Dietsch

Composed in *Syntax* and *New Century Schoolbook* by Que Corporation

We'd Like to Hear from You!

As part of our continuing effort to produce books of the highest possible quality, Que would like to hear your comments. To stay competitive, we *really* want you, as a computer book reader and user, to let us know what you like or dislike most about this book or other Que products.

You can mail comments, ideas, or suggestions for improving future editions to the address below, or send us a fax at (317) 581-4663. For the online inclined, Macmillan Computer Publishing has a forum on CompuServe (type **GO QUEBOOKS** at any prompt) through which our staff and authors are available for questions and comments. The address of our Internet site is **http://www.mcp.com/que** (World Wide Web).

In addition to exploring our forum, please feel free to contact me personally to discuss your opinions of this book: I'm **73353,2061** on CompuServe, and I'm **mpalaisa@que.mcp.com** on the Internet.

Thanks in advance—your comments will help us to continue publishing the best books available on computer topics in today's market.

Melanie Palaisa
Product Development Specialist
Que Corporation
201 W. 103rd Street
Indianapolis, Indiana 46290
USA

About the Author

Elaine Marmel is President of Marmel Enterprises, Inc., an organization that specializes in technical writing and software support and training. Elaine spends most of her time writing and is the author of several books on Word for Windows, Word for the Mac, Excel, 1-2-3 for Windows, Quicken for Windows, and Quicken for DOS. Elaine also is a contributing editor to *Inside Peachtree for Windows*, a monthly magazine published about Peachtree for Windows (an accounting package).

Elaine left her native Chicago for the warmer climes of Florida (by way of Cincinnati, OH; Jerusalem, Israel; Ithaca, NY; and Washington, D.C.) where she basks in the sun with her PC and her cats, Cato and Watson. Elaine also sings in the Toast of Tampa, an International Champion Sweet Adeline barbershop chorus.

Acknowledgments

I'd like to thank all the people who helped throughout the lifecycle of this book. Thanks to family and friends for putting up with me, and thanks to folks at Que for making it a better book.

Trademarks

All terms mentioned in this book that are known to be trademarks or service marks have been appropriately capitalized. Que Corporation cannot attest to the accuracy of this information. Use of a term in this book should not be regarded as affecting the validity of any trademark or service mark.

Contents

Part III: Making Math Easier 81

Part IV: Managing Workbooks 117

Part V: Formatting the Worksheet 137

Contents

Introduction

Microsoft Excel is one of the world's most popular spreadsheet software programs. Although you could create worksheets on ledger paper and use a calculator, and you could draw charts on graph paper, Excel makes these tasks—and others related to managing numeric information—easier. You can use the program to create worksheets, databases, and charts. Without a doubt, you could perform the following functions manually, but you can use Excel to make them easier:

- *Lay out a worksheet.* When you sit down to develop a worksheet with a pencil and ledger paper, you don't always have all the information to complete the design and layout of the worksheet. Ideas may occur to you after you sketch the layout of your worksheet. After you're finished jotting down the column headings and the row headings, you might think of another column or row you didn't include. With Excel, you can insert columns and rows easily and move information from one location to another.

- *Calculate numbers.* If you have a checkbook register, you subtract the amount of each check written and add the deposits to the running balance. If you're like me, when you receive your bank statement and balance your checkbook, you find that you made math errors in your checkbook. In your checkbook register, you must recalculate the numbers and jot down the new answers. In Excel, you use formulas, and you enter them only once. Then, when you change the numbers in the worksheet, Excel uses the formulas to recalculate the information in your worksheet. And Excel gives you the new answers instantly.

- *Make editing changes.* To correct a mistake on ledger paper, you have to use an eraser—or reconstruct the entire worksheet. With Excel, you can overwrite data in any cell in your worksheet.

- *Undo mistakes.* When you accidentally make mistakes while using Excel, you don't have to retype or reconstruct information. Instead, you can just restore the data with the Undo feature.

- *Check spelling.* Using the AutoCorrect feature, Excel corrects common spelling mistakes. And you can even add your own personal set of "common typos" to the list. In addition, before you print, you can run a spell check to search for misspellings.

- *View data.* If you were working with a large worksheet (such as a financial statement) on ledger paper, you might have to use a ruler to compare figures on a far portion of the worksheet. In Excel, you can split the worksheet into two panes to view distant figures side by side. That way, you can easily see the effects of playing "what if?" scenarios to project changes and then make the necessary adjustments.

- *Make formatting changes.* Excel enables you to align data in cells; center column headings across columns; adjust column width; display numbers with dollar signs, commas, and decimal points; format cells based on criteria you set; and apply many other formatting options. You can experiment with the settings until the worksheet appears the way that you want it. Then you can print it.

- *Change how data appears when you print.* You can make data bold, italic, and underlined. Excel also lets you shade cells, add borders, and change the typeface.

- *Preview your print job.* You can preview your worksheet to see how it will look when you print it. If you want to make changes before you print, you also can do this in print preview.

- *Sort data.* You can sort data on the worksheet alphabetically and numerically in ascending or descending order. For example, you can sort a customer invoice report in chronological order by dates. And you can use the AutoFilter feature to quickly find the top or bottom ten values in a list without sorting.

- *Chart numeric data.* You can track the sales trends of several products with an embedded column chart. Make as many "what if?" projections as you want in the worksheet by increasing and decreasing the numbers. As you change the numbers in the worksheet, Excel instantly updates the embedded chart. Excel's embedded charts let you simultaneously view the sales trends in a picture representation on-screen and the numbers in the worksheet—which makes your sales forecasting more efficient.

- *Mail workbooks.* You can easily share workbooks with colleagues. If you have access to electronic mail, you can mail workbooks from within Excel. You also can route a workbook to several different people in an order you specify.

Task Sections

The Task sections include numbered steps that tell you how to accomplish certain tasks, such as saving a workbook or filling a range. The numbered steps walk you through a specific example so you can learn the task by actually doing it.

Big Screen

At the beginning of each task is a large screen shot that shows how the computer screen will look either after you complete the procedure explained in the task or at some point during the task. (Sometimes the screen shot shows an important feature discussed in that task, such as a shortcut menu.)

TASK **4**

Using Traditional Help

"Why would I do this?"

Excel offers several approaches to getting help. In the Help dialog box, contains three tabs: Contents, Index, and Find.

Use the Contents tab to find help the same way you would use the table of contents in a book to find a subject; typically, you find a "chapter" that contains information related to the subject about which you want help, and then you start working in that chapter.

Use the Index tab to find help the same way you would use the index of a book: search for help alphabetically by subject.

The Find tab uses a more complicated method to get help, so I'm not going to cover that method in this book. In this task, you'll learn to use the traditional Help system to find out how to enter text in cells.

18

Why would I do this?

Each task includes a brief explanation of why you would benefit from knowing how to accomplish the task.

Step-by-Step Screens

Each task includes a screen shot for each step of a procedure. The screen shot shows how the computer screen looks at each step in the process. Throughout this book, you won't see the Windows taskbar; I've hidden it in order to provide you with clearer screens.

■▲●■▲●■▲●■●■

Task 4: Using Traditional Help

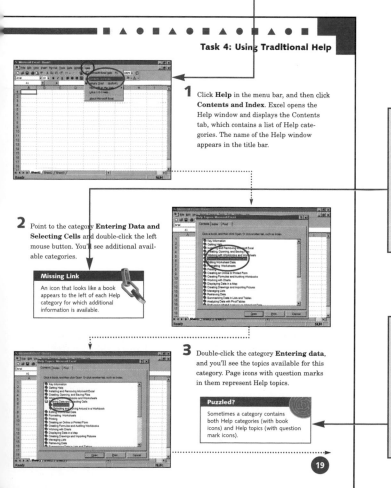

1 Click **Help** in the menu bar, and then click **Contents and Index**. Excel opens the Help window and displays the Contents tab, which contains a list of Help categories. The name of the Help window appears in the title bar.

2 Point to the category **Entering Data and Selecting Cells** and double-click the left mouse button. You'll see additional available categories.

Missing Link

An icon that looks like a book appears to the left of each Help category for which additional information is available.

3 Double-click the category **Entering data**, and you'll see the topics available for this category. Page icons with question marks in them represent Help topics.

Puzzled?

Sometimes a category contains both Help categories (with book icons) and Help topics (with question mark icons).

Missing Link Notes

Many tasks include Missing Link notes that tell you a little more about certain procedures. These notes define terms, explain other options, refer you to other sections when applicable, and so on.

Puzzled? Notes

You may find that you have actually performed a task, such as sorting data, that you didn't want to do after all. The Puzzled? notes tell you how to undo certain procedures or get out of bad situations.

19

▲●■●■▲●■▲●

PART I

The Basics

Part I OF THIS BOOK INTRODUCES you to Excel basics. You need to know some fundamental things about Excel before you start creating your own worksheets. In this part, you will learn how to start and exit Excel.

When you start the program, Excel displays a blank *workbook*. The workbook is a file in which you store your data; think of it as being similar to a three-ring binder. Within a workbook, you have sheets, such as worksheets, chart sheets, and macro sheets. A new workbook contains three sheets, named Sheet1 through Sheet3. You can have up to 255 sheets per workbook, depending on your computer's available memory. Multiple sheets help you organize, manage, and consolidate your data. For example, suppose you want to create a sales forecast for the first quarter of the year. You could place data for January, February, and March in Sheet1, Sheet2, and Sheet3 respectively; Sheet4 could contain the quarterly summary for the three months of sales data, and Sheet5 could contain a chart showing sales over the three-month period.

A worksheet is a grid of columns and rows. The rectangle that appears at the intersection of any column and row is called a *cell*. Each cell in a worksheet has a unique cell address. A cell address is the designation formed by combining the row number and column letter. For example, the cell at the intersection of column A and row 8 is called A8; that's its cell address.

The cell pointer is a cross-shaped pointer (it looks very similar to a Red Cross symbol) that appears as you slide the mouse over cells in the worksheet. You can use the mouse or the keyboard to select any cell in the worksheet. The selected cell has a dark border around it and is called the *active cell*. You always have at least one cell selected at all times.

A *range* is a group of cells. While a range can be a single cell, the term usually refers to a group of cells. A range can be a column or row of cells, or it can be any rectangular set of cells. When I talk about a range, I will refer to the range using a combination of two cell addresses. The first cell address in a range is the address of the upper-most left cell in the range; the second cell address is the address of the lower-most right cell. A colon (:) separates the two elements. So, for example, the range A1:C3 includes the cells A1, A2, A3, B1, B2, B3, C1, C2, and C3.

The Excel worksheet is much larger than your computer screen can possibly display at one time. To place data in the many cells that make up the worksheet, you must be able to move to the desired locations. There are many ways to move around a worksheet. You can use the arrow keys to move one cell at a time, or you can use the mouse to click a cell. You can also use key combinations to quickly move around the worksheet, or you can use the mouse and click the scroll bars to view parts of the sheet that aren't visible. When you move the cell pointer to a cell, that cell becomes the active cell. You can navigate around the worksheet with the following arrow keys and key combinations:

To move...	Press...
Right or left one cell	→ or ←
Up or down one cell	↑ or ↓
To the beginning of a row	Home
To the end of a row	End+→
To the first cell (A1)	Ctrl+Home
To the last cell (that contains data)	Ctrl+End

Starting and Exiting Excel

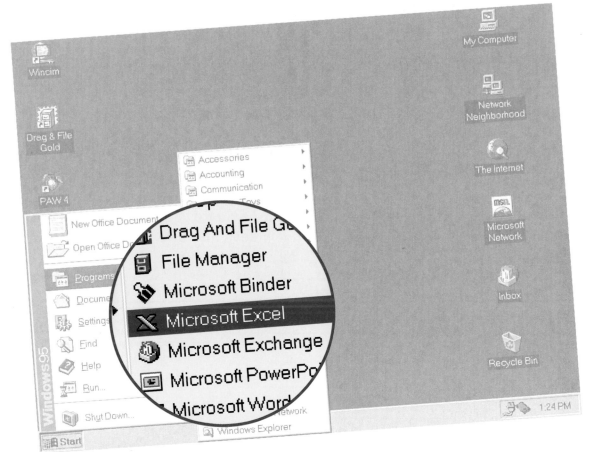

"Why would I do this?"

Starting Excel is simple to do—and it's the first, most necessary, step toward getting anything else done. Once you learn to start Excel, it's as easy as starting the engine in your car! When you no longer want to work in Excel, you can exit Excel. To start and exit Excel, you'll use menus.

To perform this task, make sure that you have installed Excel on your hard disk and turned on your computer and monitor. You'll see the Windows 95 Desktop. Note that in the pictures of Excel throughout this book, you won't see the Windows taskbar; I've hidden it to provide you with clearer screens.

10

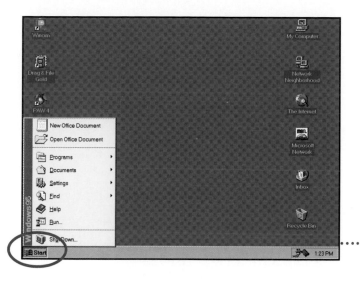

1 Click the **Start** button to display the Start menu.

2 Slide the mouse up to the **Programs** menu. Windows displays the choices available on the Programs menu, which will be different on each computer.

Missing Link

The choices on the Programs menu vary from computer to computer because they represent the software installed on each person's computer.

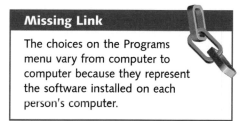

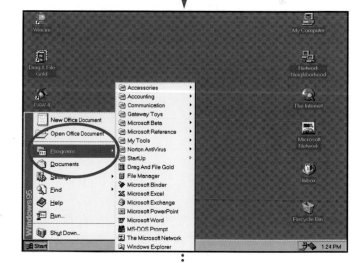

3 In the Programs submenu, click the **Microsoft Excel** icon. Excel starts, and a blank workbook appears. You may also see the Assistant (which looks like an animated paper clip) in a small window at the lower-right edge of the Excel screen. You can close the Assistant by clicking **Start Using Microsoft Excel** or by clicking the **Close** (X) button in the upper-right corner of the window. You'll learn about the Assistant later in this section.

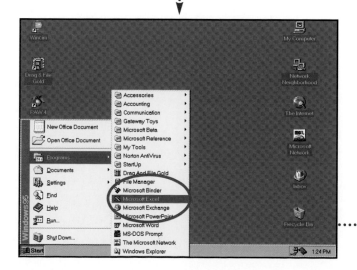

Task 1: Starting and Exiting Excel

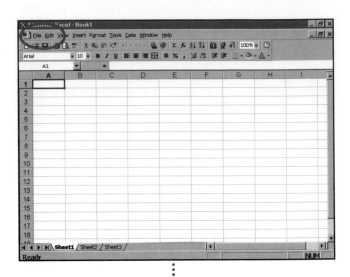

4 To exit Excel, click **File** in the menu bar. Excel opens the File drop-down menu.

Puzzled?

When you're using the mouse to start a program, make sure you click the left mouse button. If nothing happens, check the location of the mouse pointer and make sure you're pointing somewhere on the title for the program before you try clicking.

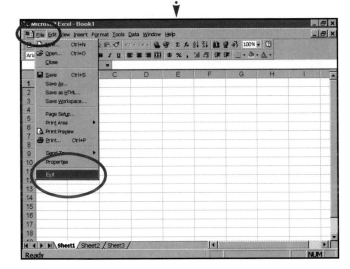

5 Click the **Exit** command to close the program and return to the Windows desktop. ■

Missing Link

To quickly exit Excel, click the **Close** button. This button, which contains an X, appears in the upper-right corner of the screen, at the left end of the Excel window's title bar.

Using Shortcut Menus

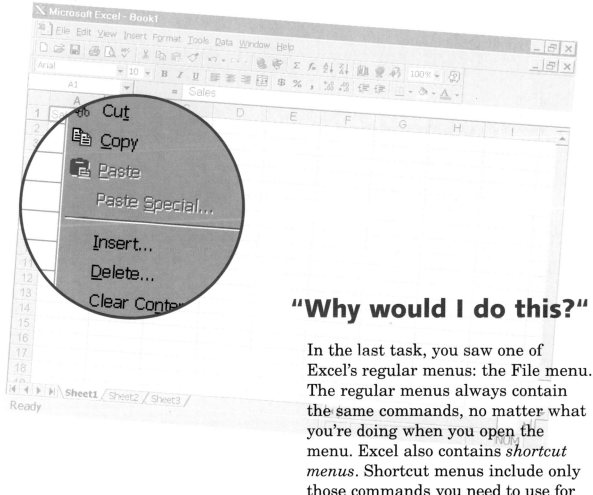

"Why would I do this?"

In the last task, you saw one of Excel's regular menus: the File menu. The regular menus always contain the same commands, no matter what you're doing when you open the menu. Excel also contains *shortcut menus*. Shortcut menus include only those commands you need to use for the currently selected cell(s) or object (such as a chart). You might want to use a shortcut menu to quickly edit or format cells.

Let's take a look at a shortcut menu that contains editing and formatting commands.

13

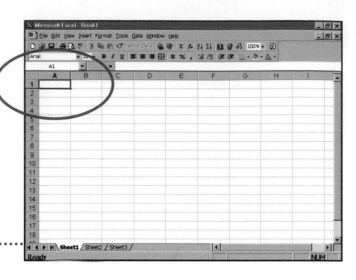

1 Start Excel. (If you need help with this step, see Task 1, "Starting and Exiting Excel.") When the blank workbook appears, the active cell will be cell A1.

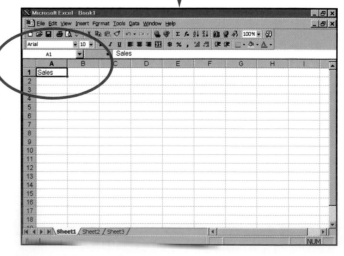

2 Type **Sales** and press **Enter**. The word "Sales" appears in cell A1, and the cell selector moves to cell A2, making it the active cell.

3 Click cell **A1**. The cell selector moves back to cell A1, making A1 the active cell again. A1 is the cell for which you want to open the shortcut menu.

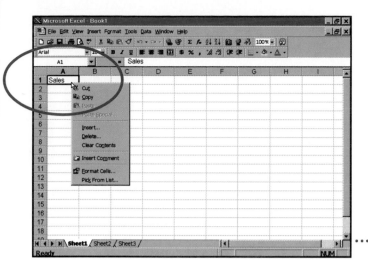

4 Point to cell **A1** and click the right mouse button. Excel opens a shortcut menu that contains a list of editing and formatting commands.

5 Click **Clear Contents** to select the Clear Contents command and erase the contents of cell A1. The shortcut menu disappears. ■

Puzzled?

Occasionally, you might display a menu or shortcut menu that doesn't have the command you want to use. To leave any menu without making a selection, press the **Esc** key or click anywhere outside of the menu. If you click a different cell, that cell becomes the active cell.

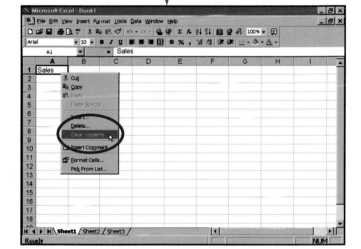

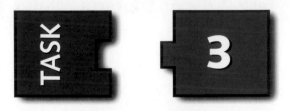

Using the Toolbars

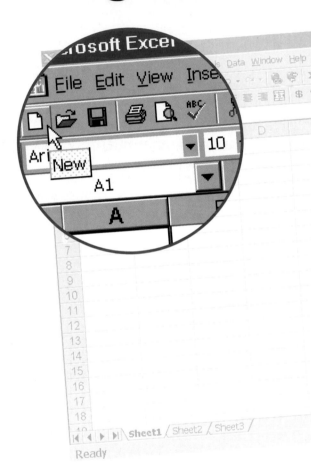

"Why would I do this?"

Toolbars appear at the top of the Excel window just below the menu bar. They contain buttons that you can use as shortcuts to bypass selecting commands from menus in Excel. To help you find the correct button, Excel groups buttons with related functions together on a toolbar. For example, the Standard toolbar contains buttons for the most common Excel commands. Similarly, the Formatting toolbar contains lists and buttons for the most common formatting commands. As you work through the tasks in this book, you'll notice that there is a different toolbar for just about every feature in Excel 97.

You must have a mouse to use the toolbars. To perform tasks quickly, you click a toolbar button instead of opening a menu and choosing a command.

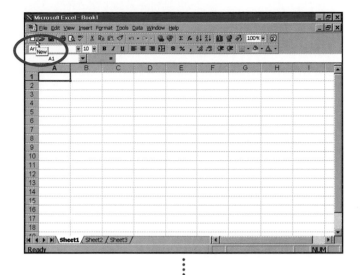

1 Point to the first button on the left on the Standard toolbar. A yellow box containing the word "New" appears near the button.

Missing Link

The yellow boxes are called ScreenTips. ScreenTips contain the name of a toolbar button and appear whenever you rest the mouse pointer on a toolbar button. If the ScreenTip does not appear, try moving the mouse pointer again and then pausing for a few seconds.

2 Click the **New** button, and Excel opens a new workbook, displaying Book2 on top of Book1. You won't be able to see Book1 anymore, but it's still there.

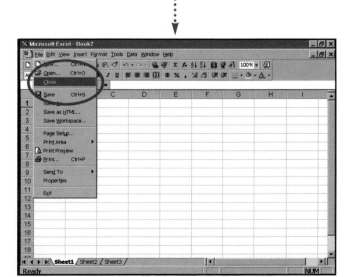

3 Click **File** in the menu bar. Notice that pictures appear to the left of some menu commands. In most cases, those pictures match buttons on the toolbars. By looking at a menu, you can tell which commands have toolbar button shortcuts. Click **Close**, and Excel closes the Book2 workbook. ■

Puzzled?

If you don't see a toolbar button, Excel may not currently be displaying the particular toolbar containing that button. Excel displays only those toolbars whose tools are useful to the task you're currently performing.

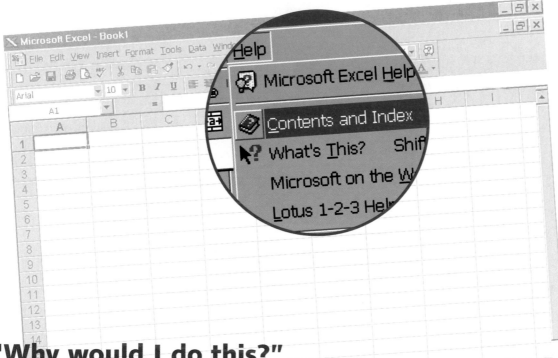

Using Traditional Help

"Why would I do this?"

Excel offers several approaches to getting help. The Help dialog box, contains three tabs: Contents, Index, and Find.

Use the Contents tab to find help the same way you would use the table of contents in a book to find a subject; typically, you find a "chapter" that contains information related to the subject about which you want help, and then you start working in that chapter.

Use the Index tab to find help the same way you would use the index of a book: search for help alphabetically by subject.

The Find tab uses a more complicated method to get help, so I'm not going to cover that method in this book. In this task, you'll learn to use the traditional Help system to find out how to enter text in cells.

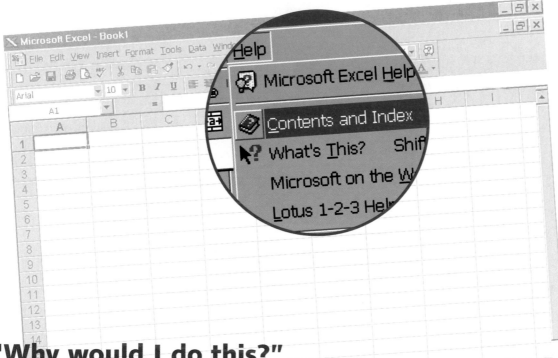

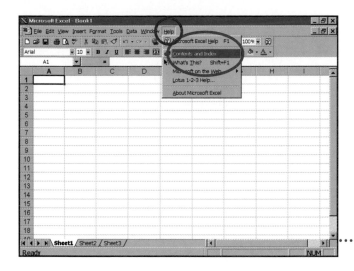

1 Click **Help** in the menu bar, and then click **Contents and Index**. Excel opens the Help window and displays the Contents tab, which contains a list of Help categories. The name of the Help window appears in the title bar.

2 Point to the category **Entering Data and Selecting Cells** and double-click the left mouse button. You'll see additional available categories.

Missing Link

An icon that looks like a book appears to the left of each Help category for which additional information is available.

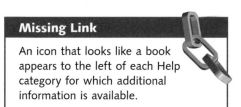

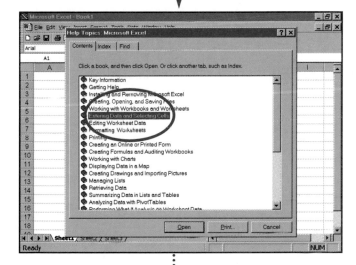

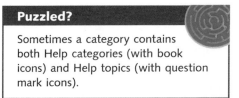

3 Double-click the category **Entering data**, and you'll see the topics available for this category. Page icons with question marks in them represent Help topics.

Puzzled?

Sometimes a category contains both Help categories (with book icons) and Help topics (with question mark icons).

4 Double-click the topic **Enter data in worksheet cells**. You'll see a window that asks what kind of information you want to enter into the worksheet and lists several types of information. Each type of information is preceded by an icon resembling a bullet.

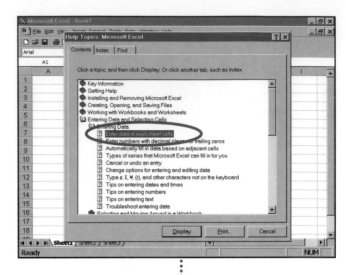

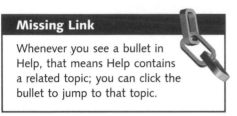

Missing Link

Whenever you see a bullet in Help, that means Help contains a related topic; you can click the bullet to jump to that topic.

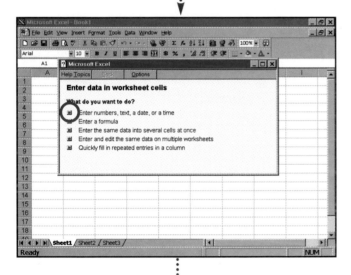

5 Click the bullet icon next to the topic on which you want help. For example, click the first bullet in the list, and you'll see a window that contains basic information on entering text or numbers, as well as related topics.

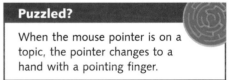

Puzzled?

When the mouse pointer is on a topic, the pointer changes to a hand with a pointing finger.

6 Click the down arrow of the scroll bar at the right side of the Help window to read more of the topic. If you see an underlined word or phrase, click it to see its definition.

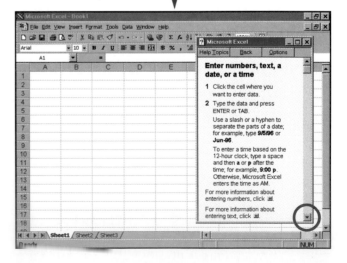

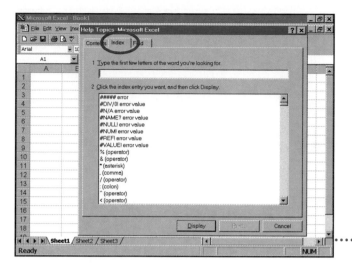

7 Suppose you want to try using the Index to get Help. Click the **Help Topics** button to redisplay the Help dialog box you saw next to step 2. Then click the **Index** tab.

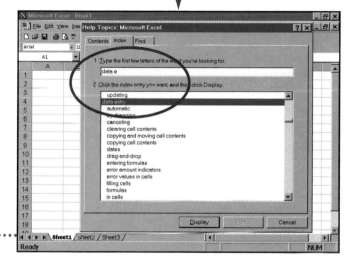

8 Type a few letters of the subject on which you want help. For example, if you type **data e** (as in this figure) Excel scrolls down the list of Help topics and highlights the first topic matching the letters you typed.

9 Scroll down the list of topics until you find one on which you want help. Highlight that topic and choose **Display**. If additional subtopics exist, you'll see the Topics Found dialog box shown here. If not, you'll see the Help dialog box that appears next to step 5. ■

Missing Link

If you click cell **A1** to select it, the Help window remains on your screen, but you can work in the worksheet. To close the Help window, click the **Close** (X) button.

Using the Assistant to Get Help

"Why would I do this?"

You can use Excel's animated Assistant as another way to get help. To use the Assistant, you ask a question, and the Assistant displays a series of choices you can click to narrow the search. Eventually, the Assistant displays a Help topic. In addition, the Assistant might occasionally pop up to let you know there is a quicker or more efficient way to perform an action that you just performed.

In the last task, you accessed the Help topic for entering text. In this task, you'll enter text and then use Excel's Undo feature to remove the entry. Then you'll display the Assistant, which will have a tip on another way to undo an entry.

Before you start, take note of the last tool on the Standard toolbar: a bubble containing a question mark. Its appearance will change as you progress through this task.

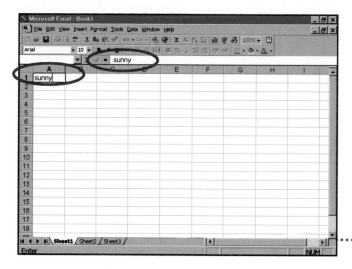

1 In cell A1, type **sunny**. As you type, the word "sunny" appears in both cell A1 and the Formula bar (just below the Formatting toolbar). Press **Enter**, and the cell pointer moves down to cell A2.

2 Open the **Edit** menu and click **Undo**. The actual wording for the Undo command changes to match the action you can undo. In this case, the entry for the command reads Undo Typing "sunny" in A1. When you select it, Sunny disappears from cell A1. Notice the light bulb in the Assistant toolbar button.

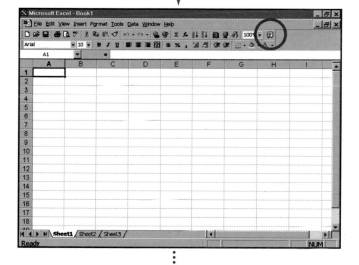

Missing Link

The light bulb appears only when the Assistant has a tip for another way to take the action you just performed.

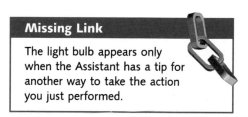

3 Press **F1**, and the Assistant appears. In the Assistant's bubble, you can type a question and click **Search** to have the Assistant look for an answer.

Missing Link

The Assistant can take on several different forms. Right-click the Assistant's window and select **Choose Assistant**. Select the **Gallery** tab and use the **Back** and **Next** buttons to see the possibilities.

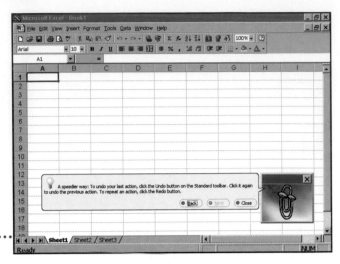

4 As an alternative, click the **Tips** button or the light bulb to display a tip. Excel displays bubble help containing a tip—in this case, a tip on how to Undo quickly and more efficiently. The Undo button appears in the bubble to help you identify the toolbar button you could have clicked.

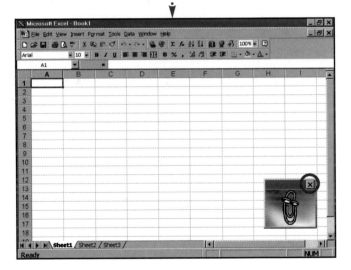

5 Click the **Close** button in the bubble, and the bubble help disappears, leaving just the Assistant. To close the Assistant, click the **Close** (X) button in the upper-right corner of the Assistant window. ■

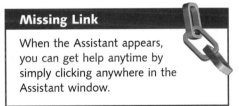

Missing Link

When the Assistant appears, you can get help anytime by simply clicking anywhere in the Assistant window.

Getting Help on Menu Commands and Dialog Boxes

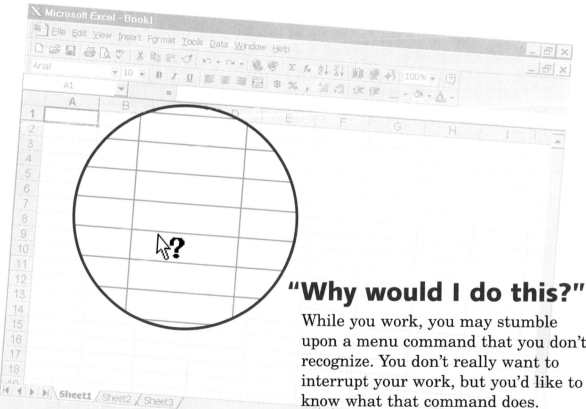

"Why would I do this?"

While you work, you may stumble upon a menu command that you don't recognize. You don't really want to interrupt your work, but you'd like to know what that command does. Similarly, you may see options in dialog boxes and wonder what those options do. But again, you don't want to interrupt your work. You can learn about these elements without stopping to access Help; use Excel's context-sensitive help instead.

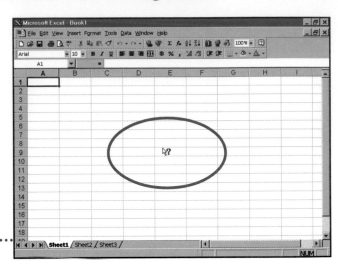

1 When you want help about a menu command, start by opening the **Help** menu and choosing the **What's This** command. Excel changes the mouse pointer shape so that it looks like a pointer with a question mark attached.

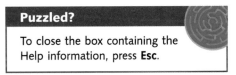

2 Open the **Insert** menu and choose the **Worksheet** command. Instead of executing that command, Excel displays help for it.

Puzzled?

To close the box containing the Help information, press **Esc**.

3 To get help on a dialog box option, start by opening that dialog box. For example, open the **Edit** menu and choose the **Go To** command. Excel displays the Go To dialog box which contains a Special command button.

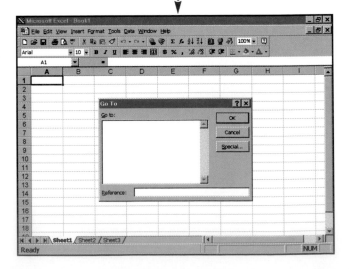

Missing Link

You can also display the Go To dialog box by pressing F5. (F5 is a shortcut key you can press to select the Go To command without opening the menu.)

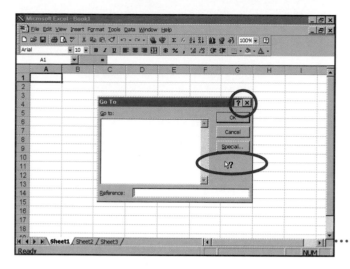

4 Click the question mark that appears in the upper-right corner of the dialog box, and again the mouse pointer changes shape to look like a pointer with a question mark attached.

5 Click the dialog box item about which you want information. For example, click the **Special** button. Excel displays a ScreenTip explaining the item. ■

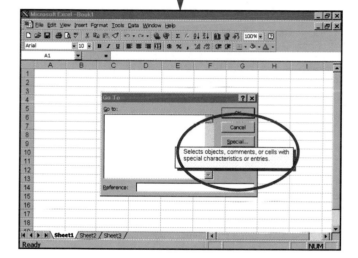

Moving Around the Worksheet

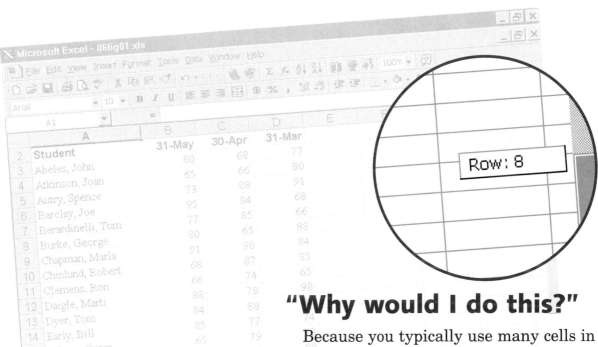

Row: 8

"Why would I do this?"

Because you typically use many cells in a worksheet and your screen can display only a limited number of them, you need shortcuts for moving around the worksheet. In the introduction, you learned some of the keyboard shortcuts you can use to move around in the worksheet; and in the last task, you learned about F5, which opens the Go To dialog box. But sometimes, using a mouse is often the easiest way to move around the worksheet; simply use the vertical and horizontal scroll bars to see other portions of the worksheet.

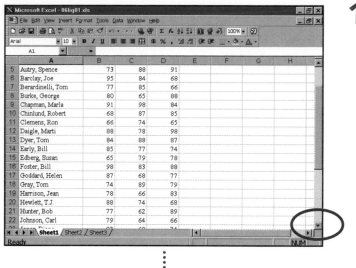

1 Click in cell **A1** and then click four times on the down scroll arrow at the bottom of the vertical scroll bar. Clicking the down scroll arrow moves the displayed part of the worksheet down one row at a time. When you stop, row 5 appears at the top of the worksheet.

Missing Link

You can point to the up, down, left, or right scroll arrow and hold down the mouse button to scroll the worksheet continuously in the corresponding direction.

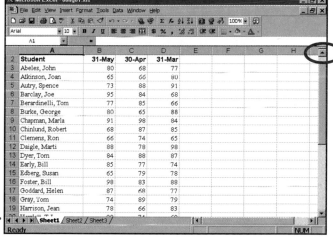

2 Click three times on the up scroll arrow at the top of the vertical scroll bar to scroll up one row at a time. Notice that in the figure, row 2 now appears at the top of the worksheet, and row 19 appears at the bottom of the worksheet.

3 Click in the vertical scroll bar itself, immediately below the solid gray scroll box. This moves the worksheet up or down one screen at a time. (After you click, row 20 will appear at the top of the worksheet, and the solid gray scroll box will be at the bottom of the vertical scroll bar.)

Missing Link

Keep in mind that whatever scroll bar action you perform on a vertical scroll bar can also be performed on the horizontal scroll bar.

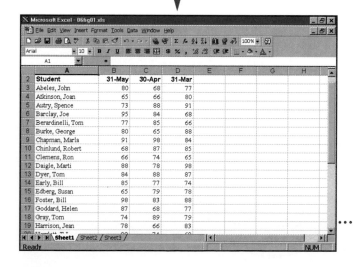

29

4 Drag the scroll box upward in the vertical scroll bar. Excel moves through the worksheet, and you see an area of the worksheet that corresponds to the location of the scroll box within the scroll bar. If you drag the box to the top, Excel moves to the beginning of the worksheet.

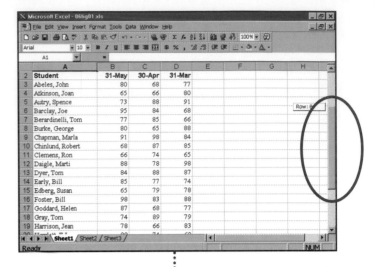

Missing Link

As you drag, a ScreenTip appears, letting you know which cell will appear at the top of the screen when you release the mouse button.

5 Move the mouse pointer to the tab split box, the vertical bar located to the left of the horizontal scroll arrow. The mouse pointer changes to a vertical bar with a left and a right arrow.

Puzzled?

If you run out of room to move the mouse on your desktop or mouse pad, just lift the mouse and then put it down in a new location. (The mouse pointer on-screen will not move when the mouse is in the air.) Then try moving the mouse again.

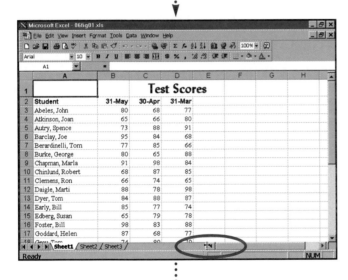

6 Drag the tab split box to the left until the box is aligned with the right edge of the Sheet2 tab. When you release the button, Excel displays fewer sheet tabs—in this case, only the tabs for Sheet1 and Sheet2. Similarly, by dragging to the right, you can display more sheet tabs. ■

Missing Link

You can double-click the tab split box to restore the sheet tabs and horizontal scroll arrow to their original positions.

Moving to a Specific Cell

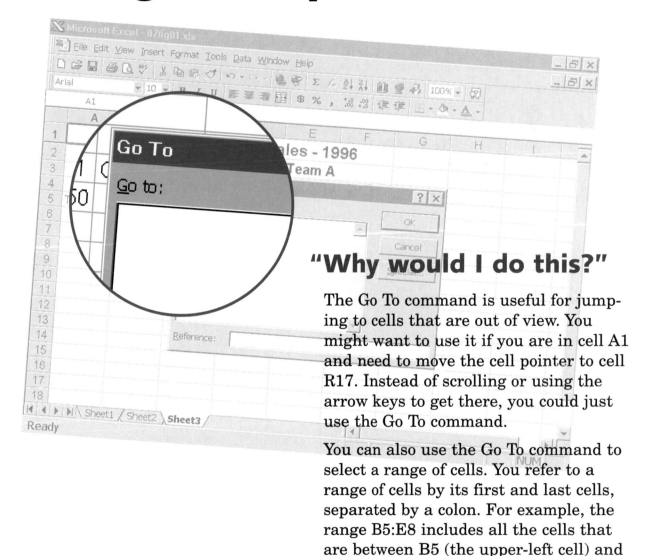

"Why would I do this?"

The Go To command is useful for jumping to cells that are out of view. You might want to use it if you are in cell A1 and need to move the cell pointer to cell R17. Instead of scrolling or using the arrow keys to get there, you could just use the Go To command.

You can also use the Go To command to select a range of cells. You refer to a range of cells by its first and last cells, separated by a colon. For example, the range B5:E8 includes all the cells that are between B5 (the upper-left cell) and E8 (the lower-right cell). This range starts with cell B5, continues across columns C, D, and E, continues down rows 6, 7, and 8, and ends at cell E8.

1 Press **F5**. F5 is the Go To key (the shortcut key for selecting the Go To command without opening the menu). Excel opens the Go To dialog box. The insertion point automatically appears in the Reference text box.

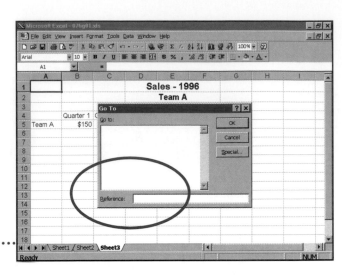

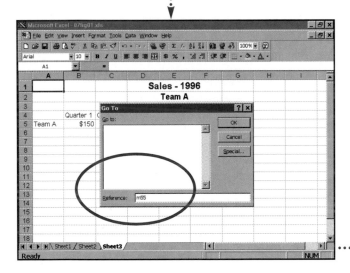

2 Type the cell address to which you want to move the cell pointer. For example, type **M55**. (Remember that you refer to a cell by its column letter and row number.)

3 Press **Enter** or click **OK**. Excel moves the cell pointer to M55, which becomes the active cell. You'll see the cell's address in the Name box near the top of the window. ∎

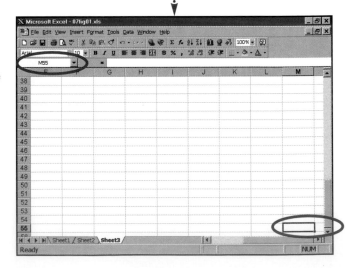

Puzzled?

If you mistakenly move to the wrong cell, repeat the Go To command to move to the correct cell. If you selected the wrong range, click any cell to clear the selection, and then try again.

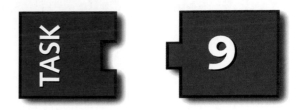
Selecting Cells

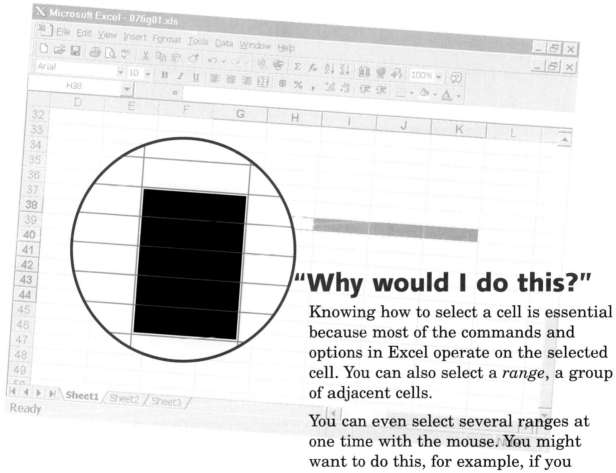

"Why would I do this?"

Knowing how to select a cell is essential because most of the commands and options in Excel operate on the selected cell. You can also select a *range*, a group of adjacent cells.

You can even select several ranges at one time with the mouse. You might want to do this, for example, if you want to perform a command on a group of cells that are not adjacent. Suppose you want to change the alignment of text in the top row of the worksheet and a column along the side. To make the change to both ranges simultaneously, you need to select both ranges at the same time.

Task 9: Selecting Cells

1 Click cell **G40** to select that cell and make it the active cell. Notice that the cell pointer outlines the selected cell, and the row and column headings for the selected cell appear in bold.

Missing Link

If, as your next action, you click cell F40, cell F40 (not cell G40) becomes the active cell. If you select the wrong cell, just click the correct cell.

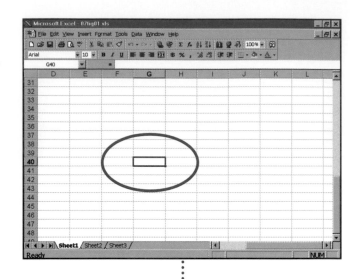

2 Hold down the mouse button, drag down the column through cells G40, G41, G42, G43, and G44, and then release the mouse button. You just selected the range G40:G44.

Missing Link

Remember, a range address consists of the address of the upper-left cell, a colon (:), and the address of the lower-right cell.

3 Hold down the **Ctrl** key and select **H38**. Then drag the mouse to select cells **I38**, **J38**, and **K38**. Release the mouse button and then release the Ctrl key. The first range (G40:G44) remains selected, and the second range (H38:K38) is also selected. If you didn't want the first range to remain selected, you wouldn't hold down Ctrl while selecting the second range. ■

Puzzled?

To select a different worksheet in the workbook, click directly on the tab of the worksheet.

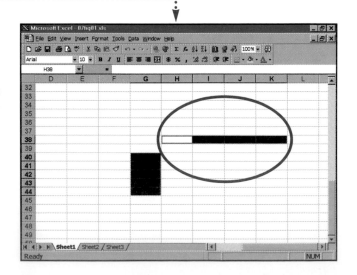

PART II

Entering and Editing Data

▲ ● ■ ▲ ● ◆ ■ ▲ ●

YOU CAN ENTER FOUR TYPES OF DATA into an Excel worksheet: text, numbers, calculations, and dates, each with its own characteristics. Text entries are sometimes called *labels*. Excel aligns labels with the left side of a cell. Labels can contain letters, symbols, numbers, or any combination of these characters. Even though a text entry may contain numbers, Excel cannot use it for numeric calculations. An example of a label is a title that describes the type of worksheet you want to create. A title such as "1994 ANNUAL BUDGET" gives meaning to the columns and rows of numbers that make up a budget worksheet. Column headings are labels that describe what the numbers in a column represent. Column headings might specify time periods such as years, months, days, or dates. Similarly, row headings are labels that describe what the numbers in a row represent. Row headings might identify income and expense items in a budget, subject titles, or other categories.

Numeric entries are also called *values*. Excel aligns values on the right side of a cell. Values contain numbers and other symbols. Numeric entries must begin with a numeral or one of the following symbols: + – (. $. The period is used as a decimal point for decimal values.

In Excel, calculations are called *formulas*. Excel displays the result of a formula in a cell as a numeric value and aligns it on the right side of a cell. You use numbers in various cells to make calculations. For instance, Excel can recognize the number in one cell, add it to the number in another cell, and display the result of the formula in a third cell.

Excel treats dates as values and aligns them on the right side of a cell. Dates in a worksheet can help you keep track of time-dependent information. For example, you can track the last time you modified your worksheet or the last time you placed a sales call. You can also enter dates in a report to show when items are posted or when transactions are done. And you can use dates in formulas to calculate, for example, the next date you want to place a sales call. Excel recognizes an entry as a valid date only if you enter the date in one of the date formats accepted by Excel. The following table shows the formats you can use when entering dates in Excel.

Format	Example
MM/DD/YY	9/12/94
DD-MMM-YY	12-Sep-94
DD-MMM	12-Sep (assumes the current year)
MMM-YY	Sep-94 (assumes the first day of the month)

Excel treats times the same way it does dates, and you can use them in the same ways you use dates. Time entries are values and appear aligned on the right side of a cell. You can use time values to create a time table or in a time study. Excel recognizes an entry as a valid time only if you enter the time in one of the time formats accepted by Excel. The following table shows the formats you can use when entering times in Excel.

Format	Example
HH:MM	13:45 (24-hour clock)
HH:MM AM/PM	2:45 AM (12-hour clock)
HH:MM:SS	13:45:06 (24-hour clock)
HH:MM:SS AM/PM	2:45:06 PM (12-hour clock)

You can enter data in an Excel worksheet using any of three methods: type the data and press Enter; type the data and press an arrow key; type the data and click the check mark in the Formula bar.

Entering Text and Numbers

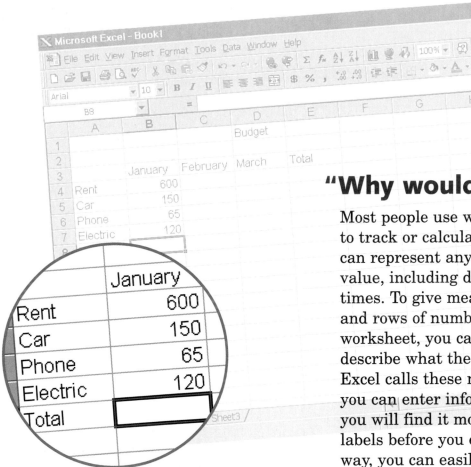

"Why would I do this?"

Most people use worksheets primarily to track or calculate numbers. Numbers can represent any kind of numeric value, including dollars, dates, and times. To give meaning to the columns and rows of numbers that make up a worksheet, you can give them names to describe what the numbers represent. Excel calls these names labels. While you can enter information in any order, you will find it most useful to enter labels before you enter numbers. That way, you can easily enter numbers into the correct cells.

The Formula bar is located beneath the Formatting toolbar near the top of the window. When you enter data in a cell, Excel displays an X and a check mark in the Formula bar. If you click the X, Excel rejects the entry; if you click the check mark, Excel accepts the entry.

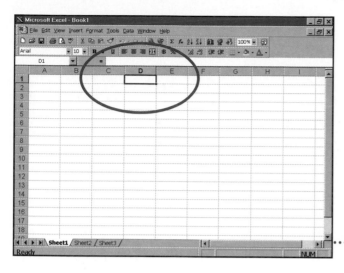

1 Point to cell D1 and click to make D1 the active cell. The active cell on a worksheet appears as a white cell with a bold border.

2 To give your worksheet a title, type **Budget**. As you type, the entry appears in the Formula bar and in cell D1. The mode indicator in the lower-left corner of the screen displays Enter.

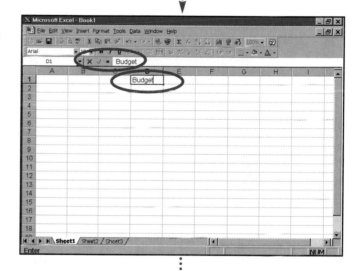

Missing Link

An X and a check mark appear to the left of the entry in the Formula bar. Clicking the X cancels the change; clicking the check mark confirms the new entry and stores the information in the cell.

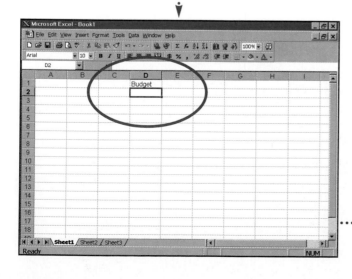

3 Press **Enter**. Excel accepts the entry and moves the cell pointer to cell D2, making it the active cell. Notice that the word "Budget" is left-aligned.

Missing Link

Excel always moves down one cell when you press Enter after typing data.

41

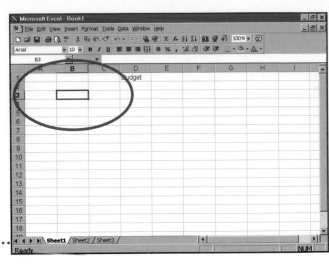

4 Select cell **B3**, in which you're going to enter a label for the first column heading.

5 Type **January** and press the right-arrow key. Pressing the right-arrow key accepts the entry, enters the label into the cell, and moves the cell pointer to the right, in this case making C3 the active cell.

Puzzled?

If you make a mistake when typing an entry, use the **Backspace** key to correct the entry. Excel does not place the entry in the cell until you press Enter, press an arrow key, or click the check mark in the Formula bar.

6 Type **February** and press the right-arrow key. Then type **March** and press the right-arrow key. Cell E3 is now the active cell.

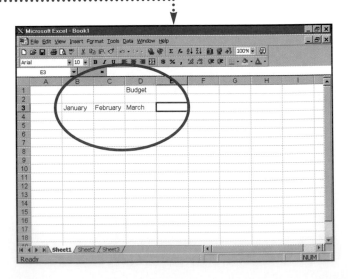

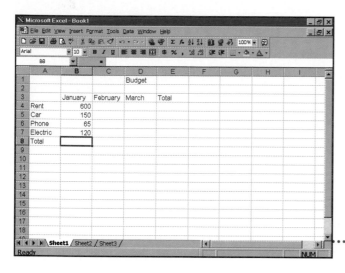

7 Type **Total** and press **Enter**. Then, starting in cell A4, type the remaining data that appear in this figure so that your computer screen matches what appears here.

Missing Link

Right up until you press Enter to accept an entry, you can press the **Esc** key or click the **X** in the Formula bar to cancel the changes.

8 Click cell **E1**, type **12-Sep**, and click the check mark in the Formula bar. Excel accepts the entry and enters the date in the cell; cell E1 remains the active cell.

Puzzled?

When you move the mouse pointer over the check mark, you might notice a ScreenTip like the one in the figure. The ScreenTip identifies the function of whatever the mouse is pointing at.

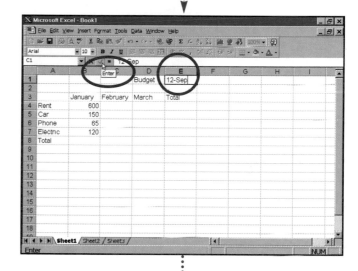

9 Click cell **F1**, type **10:00**, and click the check mark in the Formula bar. Excel accepts the entry and enters the time in the cell; F1 remains the active cell. ■

Missing Link

When you type a time or a date, it looks normal. However, when you enter it, Excel stores it in a different format. To see a date or time you've entered, highlight its cell and look in the Formula bar.

Using Undo

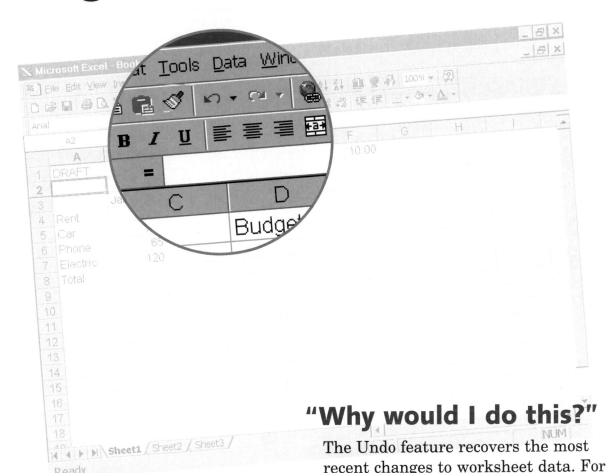

"Why would I do this?"

The Undo feature recovers the most recent changes to worksheet data. For instance, if you edit the worksheet and make a mistake, you can use Undo to reverse the last editing command you performed before you save the worksheet. Undo becomes very helpful when you need to correct editing and formatting mistakes, especially when you delete data that you did not intend to delete.

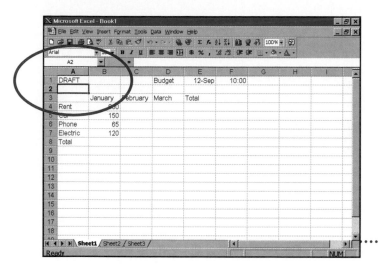

1 To see how the Undo feature works, first enter a label into cell A1. Click cell **A1**, type **DRAFT**, and press **Enter**.

2 Click the **Undo** button on the Standard toolbar, or open the **Edit** menu and choose the **Undo** command. Excel removes the entry from cell A1. ■

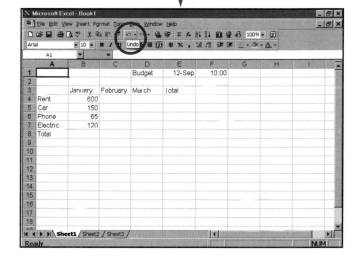

> **Puzzled?**
>
> To "undo" the Undo, click the **Redo** button immediately to the right of the Undo button on the Standard toolbar.

TASK **12**

Editing a Cell Entry

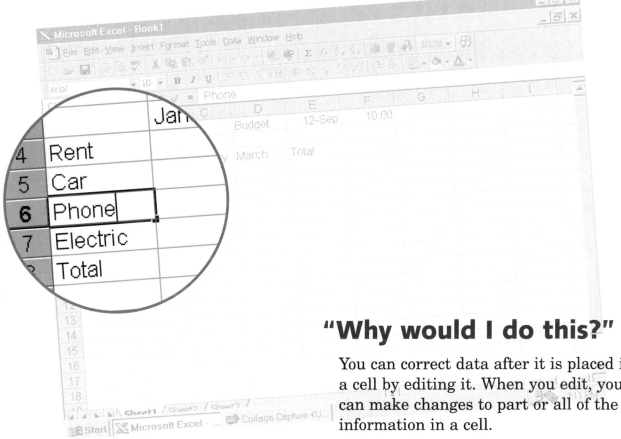

"Why would I do this?"

You can correct data after it is placed in a cell by editing it. When you edit, you can make changes to part or all of the information in a cell.

Once you know how to edit your data, you can just make a few quick changes to correct the contents of a cell. You'll save a lot of time correcting long entries because you won't have to type an entire entry over again. If the new entry is entirely different, however, overwriting the entry may turn out to be faster.

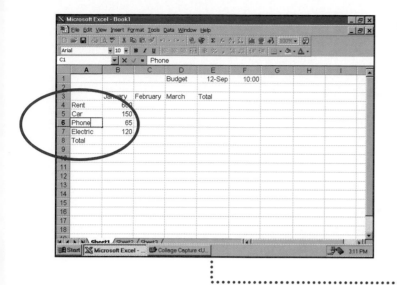

1 Double-click cell **A6** (which contains the entry you want to change) to the right of the text that appears in the cell. The X and check mark appear in the Formula bar.

Missing Link

Double-clicking a cell displays the insertion point in the cell at the location where you double-clicked. In step 1, when you click to the right of the text that appears in the cell, the insertion point appears at the end of the cell entry.

2 Press **Home** to move the insertion point to the beginning of the entry.

Missing Link

You can use the arrow keys to move the insertion point to the characters you want to change.

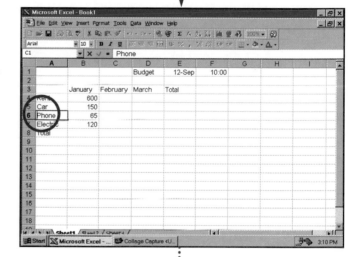

3 Type **Tele** to add those letters in front of the current label (Phone).

Task 12: Editing a Cell Entry

4 Let's change the capital P to a lowercase p. Press **Ins** (or **Insert**), and the P becomes highlighted.

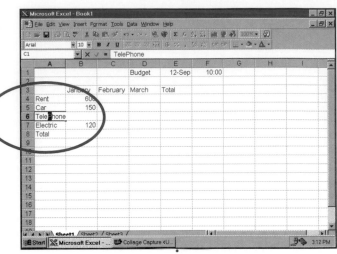

> ### Missing Link
>
> When you press **Ins**, Excel highlights the character immediately to the right of the insertion point (in this case, the letter P). Any time numbers or characters appear highlighted when you're working in Edit mode, typing will replace the highlighted character with whatever character you type.

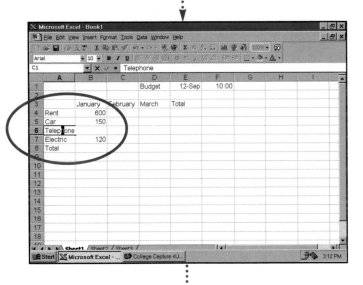

5 Type **p**. Excel replaces the highlighted letter (the capital P) with the text you typed (a lowercase p) and highlights the next letter, h.

> ### Puzzled?
>
> If you make a mistake when typing the entry in Edit mode, use the Del key or the Backspace key to correct the entry. Excel does not place the entry in the cell until you press Enter or an arrow key.

6 Press **Enter**. Excel accepts the new entry and makes A7 the active cell. ■

> ### Missing Link
>
> If the change is minor, you can edit the cell as you did in this task. Alternatively, you can overwrite the information in the cell by typing over it to replace incorrect data, or you can erase the cell's contents by selecting the cell and pressing the **Del** key.

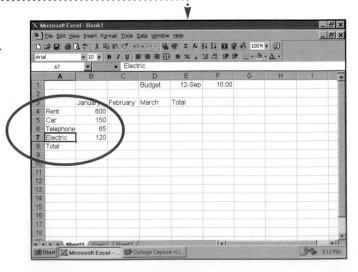

Copying or Moving a Cell Entry

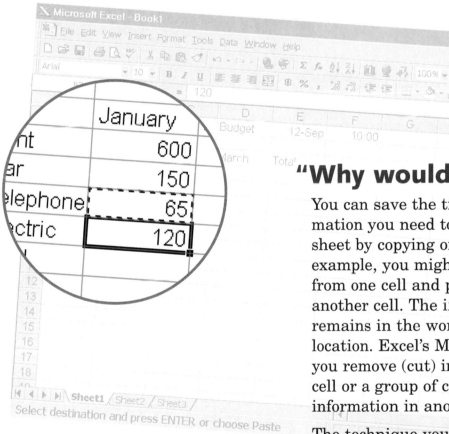

"Why would I do this?"

You can save the time of retyping information you need to repeat in the worksheet by copying or moving a cell. For example, you might want to copy a label from one cell and paste the label in another cell. The information you copy remains in the worksheet at its original location. Excel's Move command lets you remove (cut) information from one cell or a group of cells and paste the information in another location.

The technique you'll learn in this task is particularly useful if you need to copy or move information to several different locations because the technique places the information on the Windows Clipboard. Information you place on the Clipboard can be pasted repeatedly because it remains there until you replace it with something else.

49

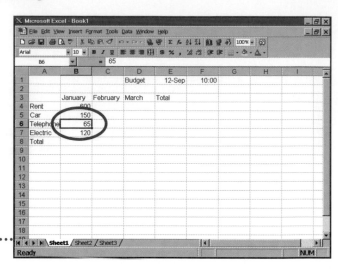

1 Select cell **B6** to make it the active cell. The Formula bar displays the current entry (the entry you want to copy).

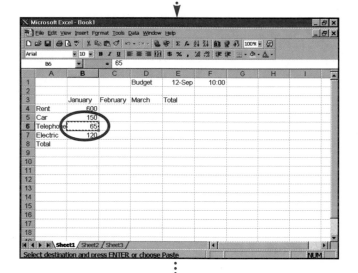

2 To copy a cell entry, press **Ctrl+C** or click the **Copy** button on the Standard toolbar. A dashed "marquee" surrounds the cell you are copying. The status bar reminds you how to complete the task: Select destination and press ENTER or choose Paste.

Missing Link

To move a cell entry instead of copying it, press **Ctrl+X** or click the **Cut** button (the scissors button) on the Standard toolbar.

3 Select cell **B7** so you can copy the information to it. Notice that the dashed marquee still appears around B6, the cell whose entry you copied.

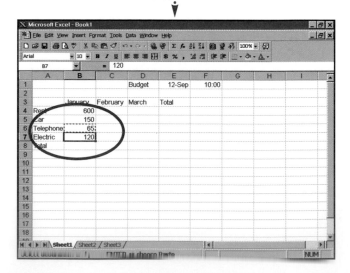

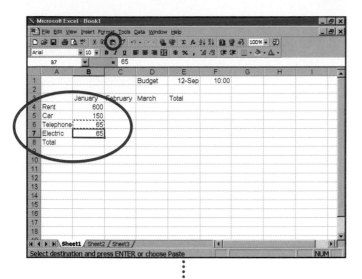

4 Press **Ctrl+V** or click the **Paste** button on the Standard toolbar to paste a copy of the data into the cell. Excel copies the entry into cell B7, retaining the applied format (alignment, protection settings, and so on). The dashed marquee remains so you can paste the data again.

Missing Link

If you had cut instead of copying, the original entry in cell B6 would have disappeared.

5 To remove the marquee when you finish copying (or cutting), press **Esc**. ■

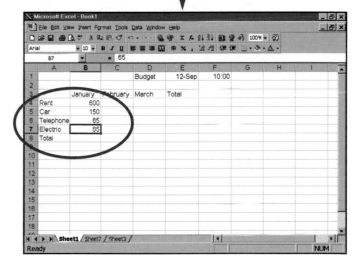

Moving and Copying Using Drag and Drop

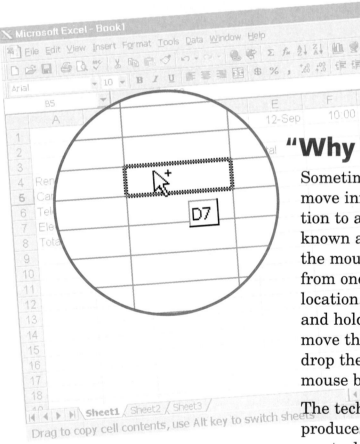

"Why would I do this?"

Sometimes you only need to copy or move information once—from one location to another. Using a technique known as "drag and drop," you can use the mouse to quickly drag information from one location and drop it in another location. To drag information, you press and hold the left mouse button and then move the mouse on your desktop. To drop the information, you release the mouse button.

The technique you learn in this task produces the same result as the previous task, but it's quicker and easier because you don't have to open menus or use keyboard shortcuts. Remember, however, that the drag and drop technique *does not* place information on the Windows Clipboard; therefore, this technique is quicker only if you need to copy or move information just once.

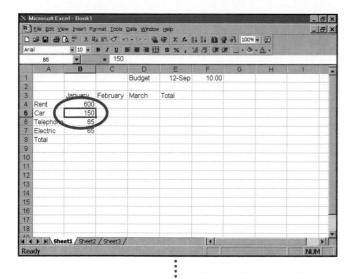

1 Click the cell containing the information you want to copy (or move). For this example, click **B5**.

Missing Link

You may find it more practical to use the traditional moving and copying techniques described in Task 14 if you need to move or copy information to a location that you cannot see while you are viewing the information you want to move or copy.

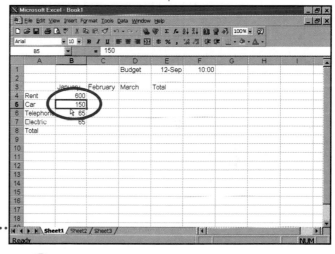

2 Place the tip of the mouse pointer on any edge of the cell. The mouse pointer's shape changes from a plus sign to an arrow pointing upward and to the left.

3 To copy information, first press and hold the **Ctrl** key and then press and hold the mouse button. When you press Ctrl, the mouse pointer's shape changes slightly: a small plus sign is attached to the arrow.

Puzzled?

To move information, do not press the **Ctrl** key when you drag. Just press and hold the left mouse button. The mouse pointer becomes an arrow, but you won't see the small plus sign.

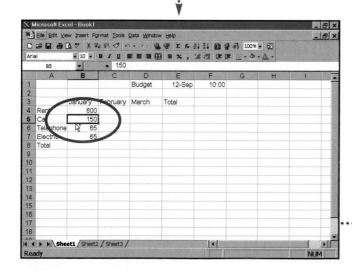

Task 14: Moving and Copying Using Drag and Drop

4 Without releasing the mouse button or the Ctrl key, drag the mouse pointer to the new location. For example, drag to **D7**. As you drag, the cell pointer outline appears shaded, and you see a box with text that changes as you move.

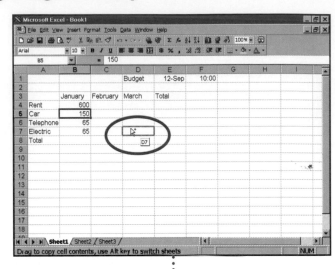

Missing Link

The box with the text is called a ScreenTip, and it contains explanatory information (in this case, the location of the cell pointer as you drag).

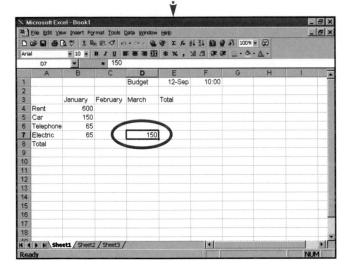

5 To complete the operation, release the mouse button and the Ctrl key. Excel copies the contents of the original cell into the new location and leaves the original cell unchanged. (If you cut, Excel removes the contents of the original cell.) ■

Puzzled?

If you "drop" the cell too soon, use the Undo feature to restore the worksheet to its original appearance, and then try again.

Filling a Range

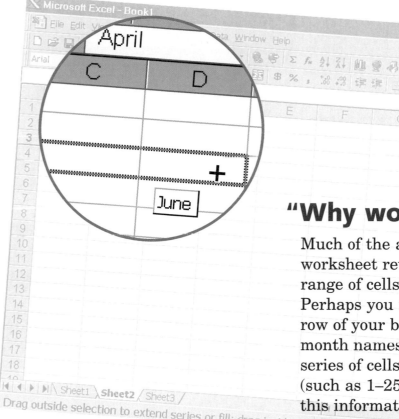

"Why would I do this?"

Much of the activity in setting up a worksheet revolves around filling a range of cells with consecutive values. Perhaps you may need to fill the top row of your budget worksheet with month names. Or you may need to fill a series of cells with consecutive numbers (such as 1–25). Of course you can type this information into the cells, but you can save yourself a lot of time by using the Fill Series command on Excel's Edit menu.

You can also use this command to fill a range with incremental values. For example, you may want the names of alternating months (instead of all twelve consecutive months) to appear at the top of your budget worksheet. The Fill Series command can also handle that task with no problem.

Task 15: Filling a Range

1 Click the **Sheet2** tab. Excel selects Sheet2 and moves it to the top, making it the active sheet. Then click cell **B3**, where you will enter the first column heading.

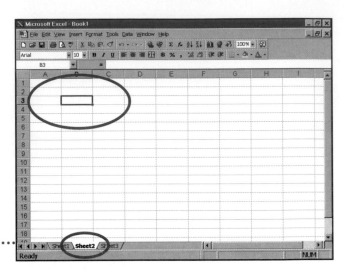

2 Type **April** and click the check mark in the Formula bar. You'll use the contents of B3 as the first value in the range; Excel calls this value the *start value*. Excel evaluates this value to determine the type of information you want to place in the range—in this case, months.

Missing Link

Excel will automatically fill the range based on the kind of data in the first cell in the range (the start value).

3 Move the mouse pointer to the lower-right corner of the current cell's border. The mouse pointer changes to a black plus sign.

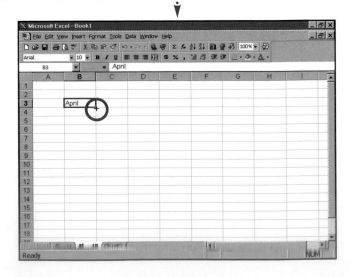

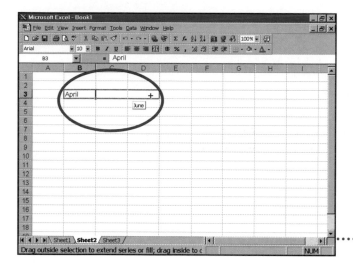

4 Drag the cell's border to include cells C3 and D3. As you drag over each cell, Excel displays a ScreenTip: you'll see the words "May" and "June" as you drag.

Missing Link

In this case, the ScreenTip indicates what will appear in the cell after you fill it.

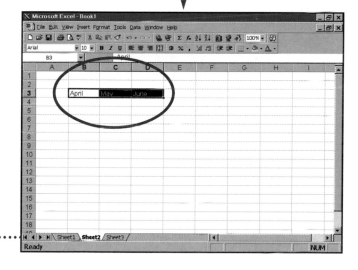

5 Release the mouse button, and Excel fills the range with months.

Puzzled?

To undo the fill series, click the **Undo** button on the Standard toolbar immediately after filling the range.

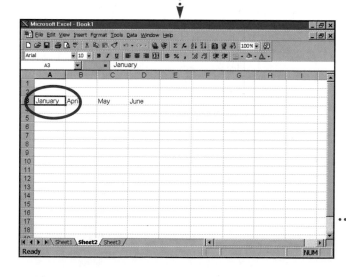

6 To fill a range with a series of incremental values, you follow the same basic steps. Type the first two values of the series into the first two cells in the range. For example, type **January** in Cell A3 and leave **April** in Cell B3. Don't worry about the contents of Cells C3 and D3; Excel will overwrite them.

7 Select both cells and move the mouse pointer to the lower-right corner of the selection's border. Again, the mouse pointer changes to a black cross.

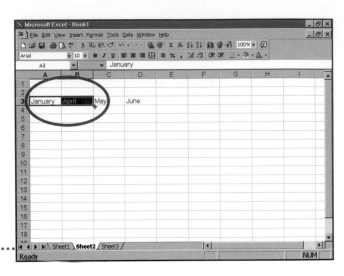

8 Drag the selection's border to include all cells in the range you want to fill: A3:D3. Again, as you drag, you'll see a ScreenTip.

9 Release the mouse button, and Excel fills the range. In this example, Excel fills cells C3 and D3 with the months July and October. ■

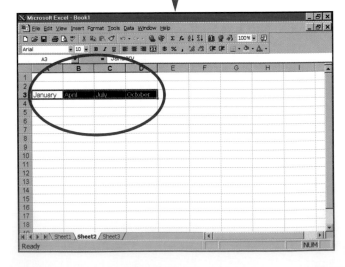

Inserting and Deleting Rows and Columns

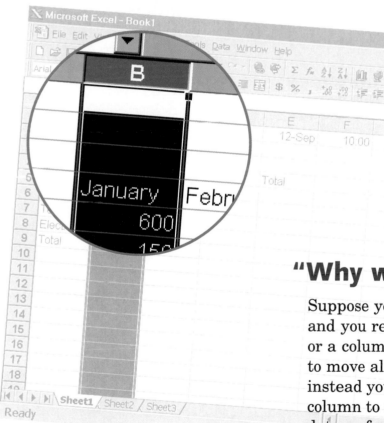

"Why would I do this?"

Suppose you're working on a worksheet and you realize that you left out a row or a column. Don't worry, you don't have to move all your information around; instead you can insert an extra row or column to make room for additional data or formulas.

On the other hand, you might find yourself wanting to delete rows or columns from a worksheet to close up some empty space. Inserting and deleting rows and columns is a painless task. To learn how to do it, go back to Sheet1 and work with the data you entered earlier.

1 Click the **Sheet1** tab, and then click cell **C2**. Excel moves to the top of Sheet1 and selects cell C2. You must select a cell so that Excel can figure out where you want to insert a new row or column.

Missing Link

Excel inserts new rows above the row that contains the selected cell; it inserts new columns to the left of the column that contains the selected cell.

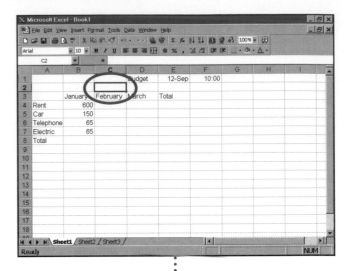

2 Click **Insert** in the menu bar and select **Rows**. Excel inserts a new row above row 2 and moves down all rows below the cell pointer. (If you had chosen Insert, Columns, Excel would have inserted a new column to the left of Column C.)

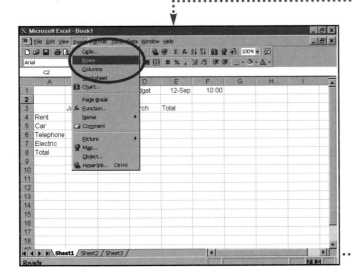

3 Next, delete a column. Click the column letter at the top of column **B** (the column you want to delete), and Excel selects the entire column. (Make sure you click the column letter, not a cell in the column.)

Missing Link

You can select an entire row by clicking the row number.

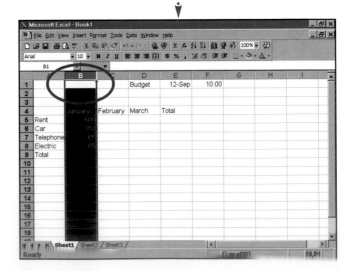

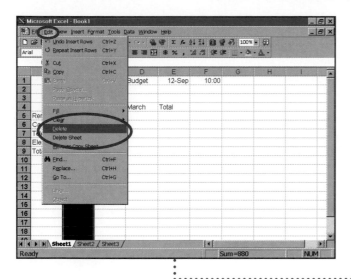

4 Click **Edit** in the menu bar and then click **Delete**. Excel deletes the column and shifts all columns located to the right of column B left one column.

Missing Link

To undo a row insertion/ deletion or a column insertion/ deletion, click the **Undo** button in the Standard toolbar.

5 Click any cell in the worksheet to clear the selection. ■

Puzzled?

If you see the Delete dialog box, you did not select the entire column. Click the **Entire Column** button and then click **OK**.

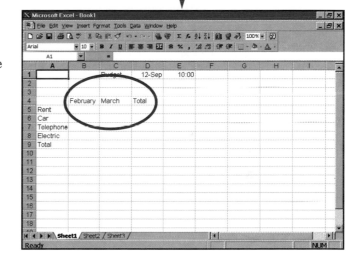

Freezing Column and Row Titles

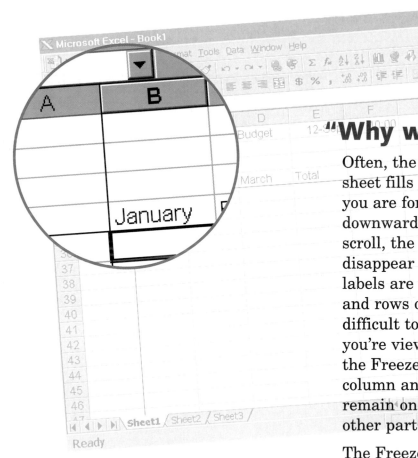

"Why would I do this?"

Often, the data you enter in a work-sheet fills more than one screen, and you are forced to scroll to the right or downward to view other areas. As you scroll, the labels you have entered will disappear from view. Because these labels are usually the titles for columns and rows of data, you'll probably find it difficult to identify the information you're viewing. However, you can use the Freeze Panes command to freeze column and row titles so that they remain on-screen when you scroll to other parts of the worksheet.

The Freeze Panes command freezes on-screen all rows above the cell pointer and all columns to the left of the cell pointer. If you want to freeze rows only, make sure the cell pointer appears in column A. Similarly, if you want to freeze columns only, place the cell pointer in row 1.

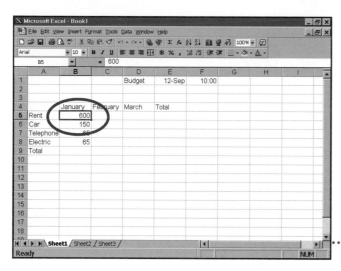

1 Click the cell where you want to freeze worksheet information. For this example, click cell **B5** to freeze rows 1–4 and column A.

2 Click **Window** in the menu bar and select **Freeze Panes**. This splits the window into panes and freezes the titles above and to the left of the active cell.

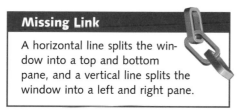

Missing Link

A horizontal line splits the window into a top and bottom pane, and a vertical line splits the window into a left and right pane.

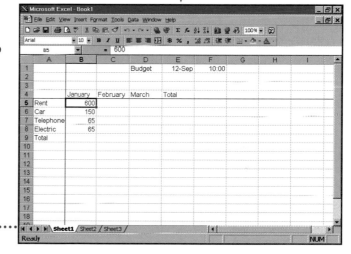

3 Repeatedly click the scroll arrow at the right edge of the horizontal scroll bar to display the far right side of the worksheet. As you can see, the row titles that appear in column A remain on-screen.

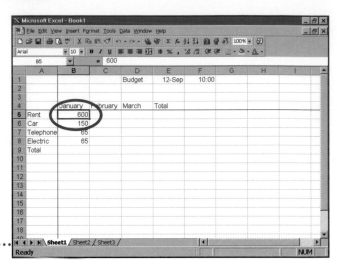

4 Press **Ctrl+Home** to return the cell pointer to the location in which it appeared when you chose the Freeze Panes command.

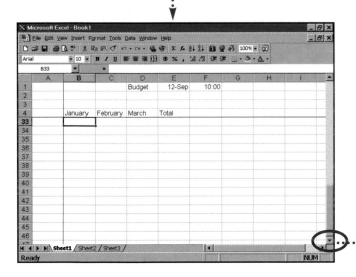

5 Repeatedly click the scroll arrow at the bottom edge of the vertical scroll bar to display the bottom portion of the worksheet. As you can see, the column titles remain on-screen.

6 Click **Window** in the menu bar and select **Unfreeze Panes**. Excel restores the worksheet to the original display. ■

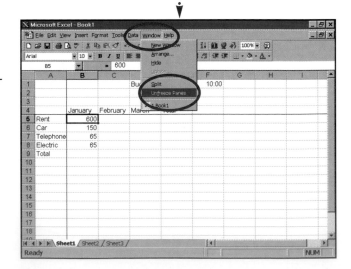

Puzzled?

If you freeze the panes in the wrong place, simply reopen the **Window** menu and choose the **Unfreeze Panes** command. Then try again.

Hiding and Displaying Columns and Rows

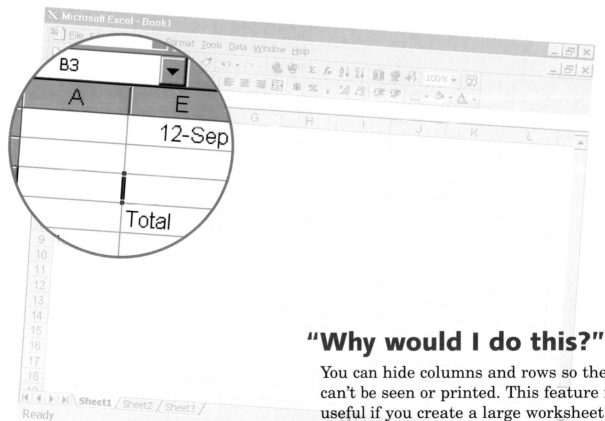

"Why would I do this?"

You can hide columns and rows so they can't be seen or printed. This feature is useful if you create a large worksheet and don't need to see certain portions of it while you work. Or perhaps you work with sensitive data and you do not want other people to see information on your screen or printout. Don't worry. When you hide columns or rows, the formulas that use data in the hidden columns continue to work properly.

1 Select a cell in each column you want to hide. For example, if you want to hide columns B, C, and D, select a cell in each.

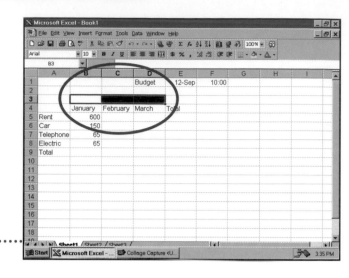

Missing Link

Excel does not allow you to hide only part of a column.

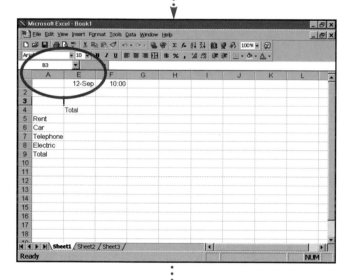

2 Click **Format** in the menu bar, click **Column**, and then click **Hide**. Excel hides the selected columns. Looking at the figure, you can tell by the column letters (A, E, F) that columns B, C, and D are hidden.

Missing Link

If you move the cell pointer after you perform step 2, you must select a range that includes the hidden columns before you perform step 3.

3 To redisplay the hidden columns, click **Format** in the menu bar, click **Column**, and then click **Unhide**. Excel redisplays the hidden columns. ■

Puzzled?

If you hide the wrong columns, click the **Undo** button on the Standard toolbar to redisplay the columns you just hid.

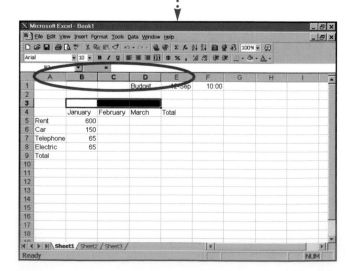

Sorting Data

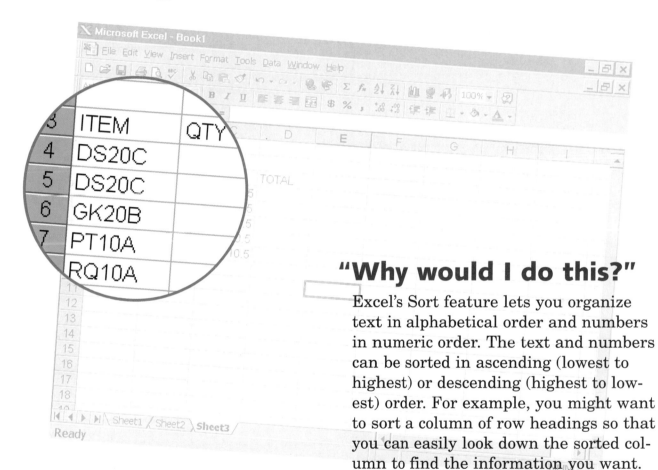

"Why would I do this?"

Excel's Sort feature lets you organize text in alphabetical order and numbers in numeric order. The text and numbers can be sorted in ascending (lowest to highest) or descending (highest to lowest) order. For example, you might want to sort a column of row headings so that you can easily look down the sorted column to find the information you want.

When you sort information that contains both text and numbers in ascending order, Excel places the numbers before the text in the list. You can sort by any column, and you can sort more than one column at a time; for complete information on these options, see your Microsoft Excel documentation.

Task 19: Sorting Data

1 Click the **Sheet3** tab. Then start in cell A1 and type the data that appears in the figure shown here. When you finish, your computer screen should match the figure in the book.

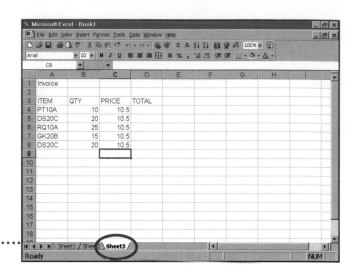

2 Drag the mouse over the range **A4:C8** to select it. Be sure to select all the data in the rows, or the entries will be mismatched. Be sure not to select the column headings.

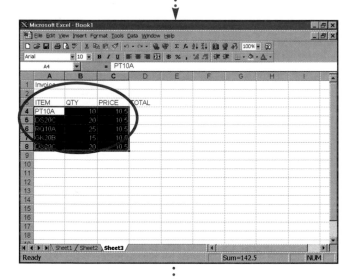

Missing Link

Note that you can also select A4:C8 by selecting cell **A4**, holding down the **Shift** key, and moving the cell pointer to cell **C8**.

3 Click the **Sort Ascending** button on the Standard toolbar. Then click any cell to clear the selection. Excel sorts the data in alphabetical order according to the item names. ■

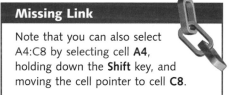

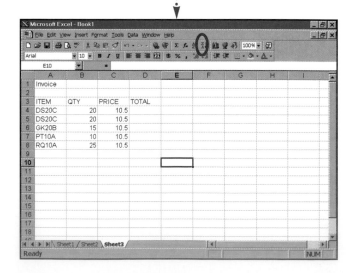

Puzzled?

If the sort does not work as you planned, immediately click the **Undo** button on the Standard toolbar or select **Edit**, **Undo Sort** to restore the range to its original order.

Filtering a List of Information

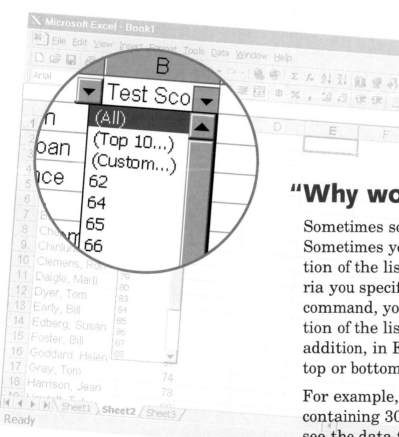

"Why would I do this?"

Sometimes sorting just isn't enough. Sometimes you want to see only a portion of the list that meets certain criteria you specify. Using Excel's AutoFilter command, you can specify just the portion of the list you want to view. In addition, in Excel 97, you can view the top or bottom numbers in the list.

For example, suppose you have a class containing 30 students and you want to see the data for the top 10 students based on the last test scores. You would set up a worksheet like the one in these figures and use Excel's AutoFilter command to hide information about the students who are not among the top 10; that way you view only a specified portion of the class list.

Task 20: Filtering a List of Information

1 Set up your worksheet so that it contains all the information you want to store. In the example shown here, the data is stored in cells A1 through B32.

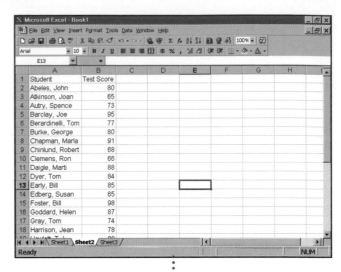

Missing Link

Keep in mind that you can filter by any column and more than one column. For complete information on these options, see your Microsoft Excel documentation.

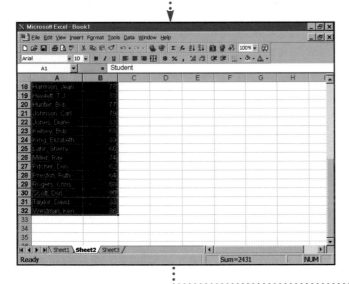

2 Drag the mouse over all the data to select it. For example, select the range **A1:B32**. Be sure to select all the data in the rows, or the entries will be mismatched.

Missing Link

You also can select A1:B32 by selecting cell **A1**, holding down the **Shift** key, and pressing the right-arrow key, the **End** key, and then the down-arrow key.

3 From the menu bar, choose **Data**, **Filter**, **AutoFilter**. Excel adds list box buttons to the first entry in each column of the selected data.

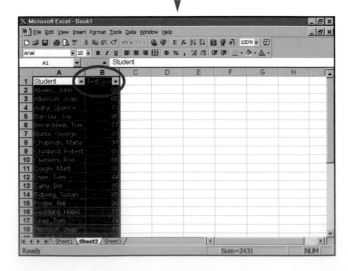

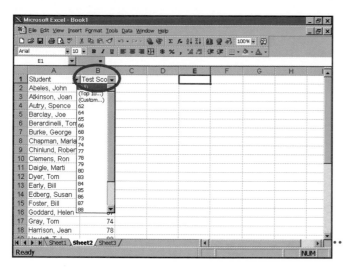

4 Click the **Test Scores** drop-down arrow. Excel shows you a drop-down list that contains the choices you have for filtering the list to display only those items you want to see.

5 Choose **Top 10**, and Excel displays the Top Ten AutoFilter dialog box. From this dialog box, open the first list box and choose **Top**. In the second text box, choose **10**; in the third text box choose **Items**.

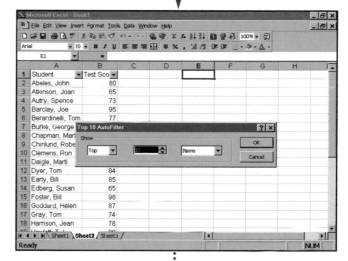

Missing Link

In the Top Ten AutoFilter dialog box, you can also choose to view the bottom portion of the list, choose to view more or less than 10 items, or choose to view items that fall within a percentage.

6 Click **OK**. Excel displays the list of items that meet the criteria you set. ■

Puzzled?

If you don't see the list you expected to see, reopen the **Test Scores** list box and choose **(All)** from the top of the list. Excel will redisplay the entire list, and you can try again. To remove the list box buttons from the tops of the columns, choose **Data**, **Filter**, **AutoFilter** again.

Finding and Replacing Data

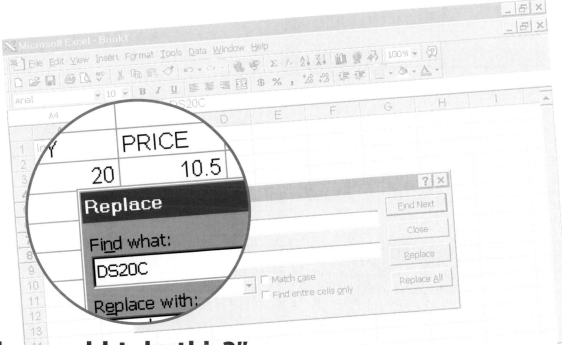

"Why would I do this?"

With Excel's Find and Replace features, you can locate certain data and then replace that original data with new data.

Suppose, for example, that you have a label, a value, or formula that you entered incorrectly throughout the worksheet. You can open the Edit menu and choose the Replace command to search and replace all occurrences of the incorrect information with the correct data.

As you'll see in this task, the Find and Replace dialog boxes allow you to tell Excel to search either in row order or column order. In addition, you can reduce the number of entries that Excel finds in two ways: you can tell Excel to match the case (upper and lower) of the characters you type in the Find What box, or you can tell Excel to include only those cells whose entire contents completely match the characters you type in the Find What box.

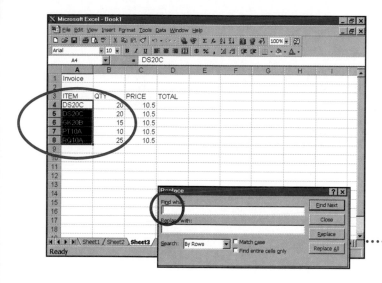

1 Drag the mouse over the cells you want to search to select them. For example, select cells **A4** through **A8**. If you want to search the entire worksheet, select cell **A1**.

2 Open the **Edit** menu and choose the **Replace** command. Excel displays the Replace dialog box, with the insertion point in the Find What text box.

3 Type the text you want to find and replace. For example, type **DS20C**. Click in the **Replace With** text box or press the **Tab** key, and then type the information you want to use as a replacement. For example, type **AB44F**.

Missing Link

The case you use when you type *does* matter. Excel will replace existing uppercase text with lowercase text if you type lowercase text in the Replace With text box.

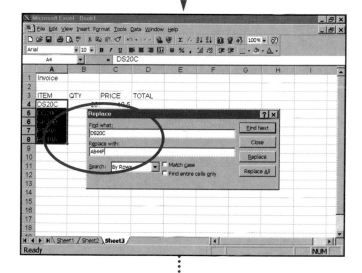

4 Click the **Replace All** button to begin the search. When Excel finishes replacing all occurrences, click outside the range to clear the selection. In this example, Excel replaced all occurrences of DS20C with AB44F. ■

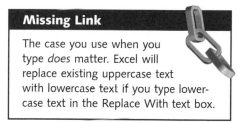

Missing Link

Make sure you really do want to replace all occurrences before you select the Replace All button. If you're not sure, search for and replace one occurrence at a time using the **Replace** button.

Checking Your Spelling

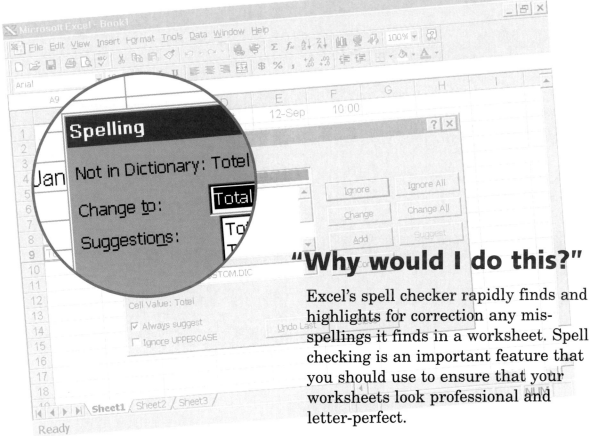

"Why would I do this?"

Excel's spell checker rapidly finds and highlights for correction any misspellings it finds in a worksheet. Spell checking is an important feature that you should use to ensure that your worksheets look professional and letter-perfect.

As you use the Spell checking feature, Excel will suggest changes to you for words it finds that it doesn't recognize. You'll have the option of accepting or ignoring Excel's suggestion. Even though spell checking can save you time, you really should proofread your work, too. Spell checkers will not report context errors and will permit mistakes such as "three" for "there."

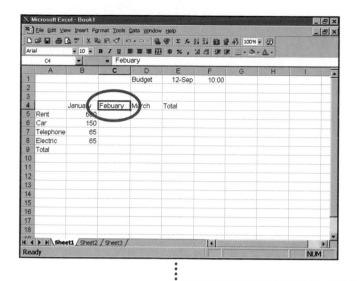

1 Click the **Sheet1** tab. If you've been following along with the examples in this book, the worksheet should look like the one shown in this figure. Go to cell **C4** and remove the first r from the word "February."

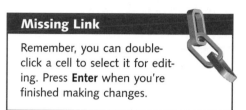

Missing Link

Remember, you can double-click a cell to select it for editing. Press **Enter** when you're finished making changes.

2 In cell **A9**, change the a in the word "Total" to an e.

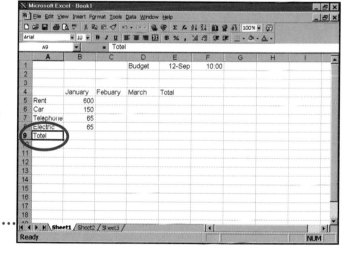

3 Select a cell to indicate what part of the worksheet you want to spell check. For this example, select **A1**. When you select the first cell in the worksheet, Excel begins spell checking at the top of the worksheet and checks the whole thing.

4 To begin the spell checker, click the **Spelling** button on the Standard toolbar. Excel finds the first misspelled word (Febuary) and displays it at the top of the Spelling dialog box. The correct spelling (February) appears in the Change To box and in the Suggestions list.

5 Click **Change**, and Excel replaces the incorrect word with the correct word in the worksheet. The spell checker automatically continues searching.

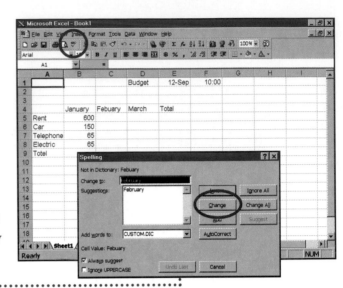

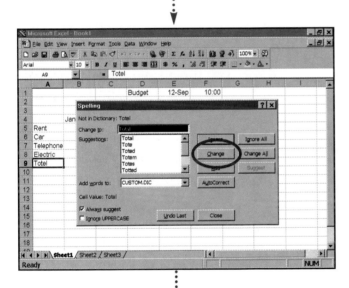

6 The spell checker displays the word "Totel" at the top of the Spelling dialog box. Click **Change**. Again, Excel replaces the incorrect word with the correct word.

Puzzled?

If the first word in the Suggestions list is not the word you need, click the down scroll arrow in the Suggestions list to find the correct word. When you see the word, click it. Excel displays it in the Change To box.

7 When Excel finishes the spelling check, it displays a dialog box that tells you spell checking is complete. Click **OK**, and you can see the corrected spellings of "February" in cell C4 and "Total" in cell A9. ■

Puzzled?

If you mistakenly select the wrong option in the Spelling dialog box, you can click the **Undo Last** button to reverse the change.

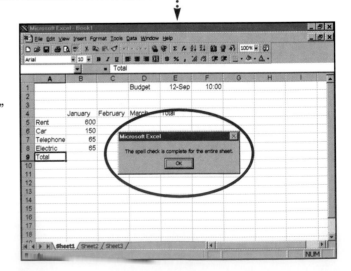

Using AutoCorrect

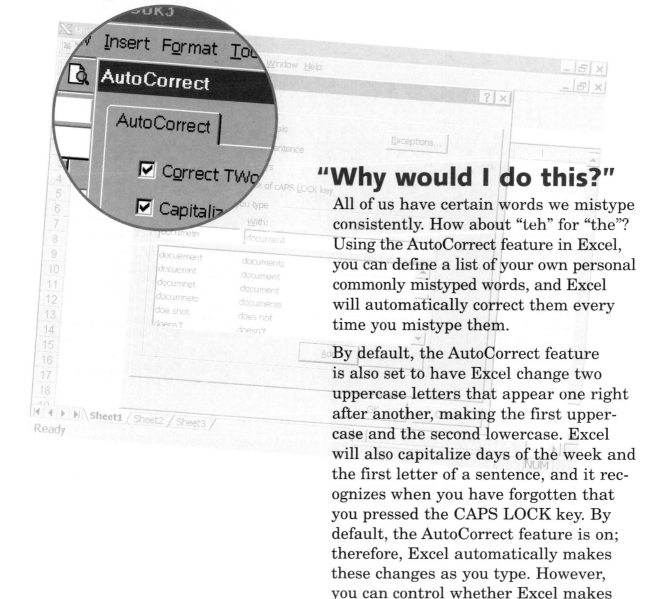

"Why would I do this?"

All of us have certain words we mistype consistently. How about "teh" for "the"? Using the AutoCorrect feature in Excel, you can define a list of your own personal commonly mistyped words, and Excel will automatically correct them every time you mistype them.

By default, the AutoCorrect feature is also set to have Excel change two uppercase letters that appear one right after another, making the first uppercase and the second lowercase. Excel will also capitalize days of the week and the first letter of a sentence, and it recognizes when you have forgotten that you pressed the CAPS LOCK key. By default, the AutoCorrect feature is on; therefore, Excel automatically makes these changes as you type. However, you can control whether Excel makes these changes by turning off some or all of the AutoCorrect options.

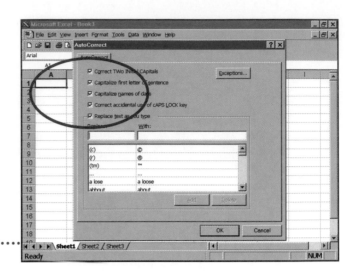

1 Open the **Tools** menu and choose the **AutoCorrect** command. Excel displays the AutoCorrect dialog box. To change the default operation of the AutoCorrect feature, click any of the check boxes to remove the checks.

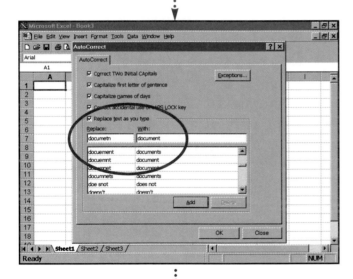

2 Excel refers to the list at the bottom of the box and replaces the specified typographical errors as you type. To add a typographical error to the list, type the wrong spelling in the **Replace** text box. Then type the correct spelling in the **With** box. Click **Add** or press **Enter** to place your typographical error in the list.

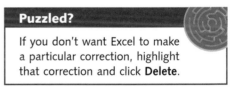

Puzzled?

If you don't want Excel to make a particular correction, highlight that correction and click **Delete**.

3 When you finish, click **OK**. ■

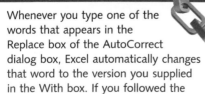

Missing Link

Whenever you type one of the words that appears in the Replace box of the AutoCorrect dialog box, Excel automatically changes that word to the version you supplied in the With box. If you followed the example in this task, try typing "docuemtn" to see how it works.

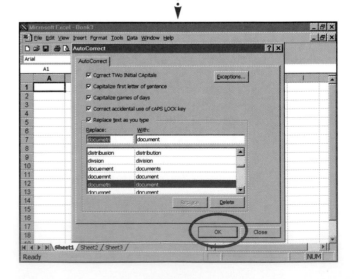

PART III

Making Math Easier

I'T'S TIME TO LEARN ABOUT USING WORKSHEETS to make math easier. In Excel, you use *formulas* to add, subtract, multiply, and divide numbers and *functions* to total cells and calculate averages.

Formulas use cell references to calculate the values in other cells of the worksheet. Once you enter a formula, you can change the values in the referenced cells, and Excel automatically recalculates the formula's value to reflect the cell changes. You can include any cells in your formula, and the cells do not have to be next to each other. Also, you can combine mathematical operations, as in the example C3+C4*D5.

Functions are abbreviated formulas that perform a specific operation on a group of values. Excel provides more than 250 functions that can help you with tasks ranging from determining loan payments to calculating the natural logarithm of a number; for example, the SUM function is particularly useful when you need to add a column of numbers.

The format for entering any function is basically the same: you start with an equal sign (=) to tell Excel you're entering a function, and then you type the function name, enclosing any arguments in parentheses. For example, the SUM function consists of the function name, SUM, and the range of cells you want to add, which you enter within parentheses.

Arguments are the parameters (such as a range containing values) that Excel needs to make the calculation.

The AVERAGE function is a predefined formula that calculates the average of a list of numbers using the method you learned in high school: the AVERAGE function adds the values you specify in a range and then divides the sum by the number of values in the range. You can use the Paste Function button (the one on the Standard toolbar with **fx** on it) to help you enter the AVERAGE function so you don't have to type it.

In fact, the Paste Function button can help you create any function, and it is particularly helpful when you are unsure of the correct syntax for the function.

For information on creating complex formulas, the order of precedence (the order in which Excel evaluates formulas), and functions, refer to your Microsoft Excel documentation.

In Excel, there are three types of cell references: relative, absolute, and mixed. The type of cell reference you use in a formula determines how Excel changes the formula when you copy it into a different cell. The formulas you create in this section contain *relative cell references*. When you use relative cell references and copy a formula from one cell to another, the cell references in the formula change to reflect the new location of the formula. Because relative cell references "adjust" to their current location, you can create a formula in Column A that adds numbers in Column A, and then copy that formula to Column B, and Excel will adjust the formula to add the corresponding numbers in Column B.

When you use an *absolute cell reference* in a formula, you force Excel to use the same cell reference even if you copy the formula. In certain formulas that you create, you may want an entry to always refer to one specific cell value. For example, when showing sales by region, you might want to calculate each region's percentage of total sales. The formula for this calculation would be the region's sales divided by total sales (and that value would be multiplied by 100 to represent a percentage). The cell address for the total sales amount must remain unchanged—absolute—as you calculate each region's percentage of total sales. So in the formula that calculates each region's percentage of total sales, you use an absolute cell reference when referring to the cell containing total sales. When you copy this formula, the total sales cell reference always refers to the one cell that contains the total sales for all regions.

A *mixed cell reference* in a formula contains both a relative and an absolute cell reference. It's helpful to use a mixed cell reference when you need a formula that always refers to the values in a specific column, but when the values in the rows must change (or vice versa).

TASK 24

Adding and Subtracting Data with a Formula

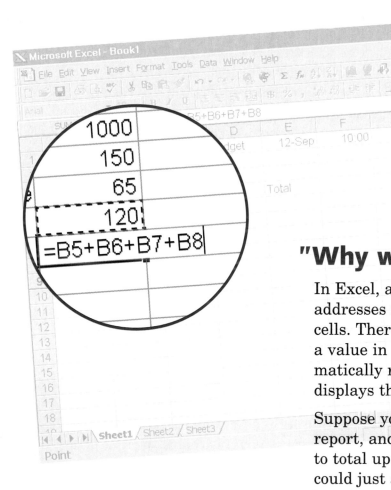

"Why would I do this?"

In Excel, a formula refers to cell addresses instead of the values in the cells. Therefore, whenever you changed a value in one of the cells, Excel automatically recalculates the formula and displays the new result.

Suppose you're filling out an expense report, and you want to enter a formula to total up your expenses. Sure, you could just add the values in the cells, but then if you had to change any of the values, Excel wouldn't update the formula you created to represent the sum of your expenses. Learn how to enter addition and subtraction formulas by creating a balance sheet.

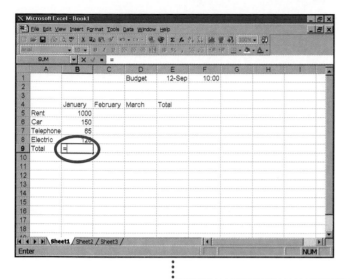

1 Enter the information shown in the figure, and then click cell **B9** to place a formula in it. (Excel will display the result of the formula.) Type **=** (the equal sign).

Missing Link

Typing = tells Excel that you're going to create a formula. You then select the cells you want to include in the formula.

2 Next you select the cells you want to include in the formula. For this example, click cell **B5**. Excel surrounds the cell with a dashed marquee and displays =B5 in both the Formula bar and cell B9.

Puzzled?

If you make a mistake typing, use the **Backspace** and **Delete** keys to correct the mistake. If you click the wrong cell, just click the correct cell to move to it.

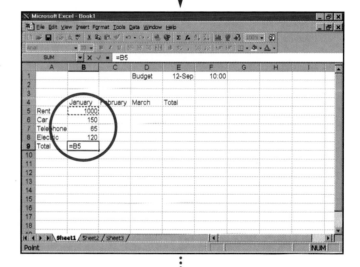

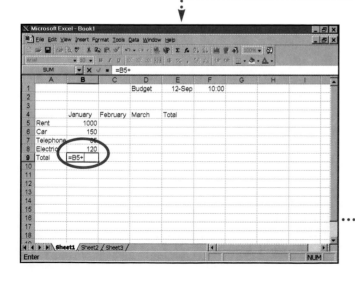

3 Type a mathematical operator, in this case the **+** sign. This tells Excel which mathematical operation you want to perform (such as addition). Now Excel displays =B5+ in the Formula bar and in cell B9. The cell pointer returns to B9.

85

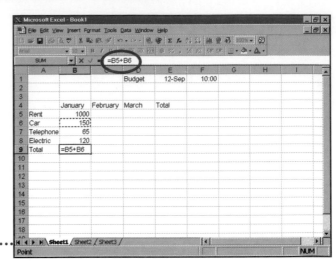

4 Click the second cell you want to include in the addition formula: cell **B6**. A dashed marquee surrounds the cell, and =B5+B6 appears in the Formula bar and in cell B9.

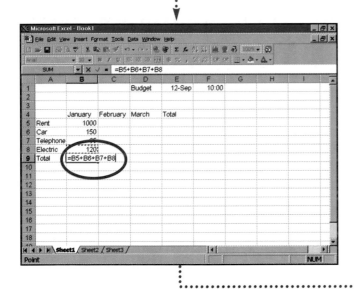

5 Repeat steps 3 and 4 to include cells B7 and B8 in your formula. (Cell B8 is the last cell you want to include in the addition formula.) You now see =B5+B6+B7+B8 in the Formula bar and in cell B9; your worksheet should look like the one shown here.

6 Press **Enter** when you finish creating the formula. You see the result of the formula (1335) in cell B9. However, anytime B9 is the active cell, the formula =B5+B6+ B7+B8 appears in the Formula bar.

> **Puzzled?**
>
> Immediately after entering a formula, you can delete it by clicking the **Undo** button on the Standard toolbar.

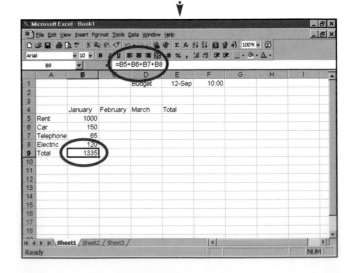

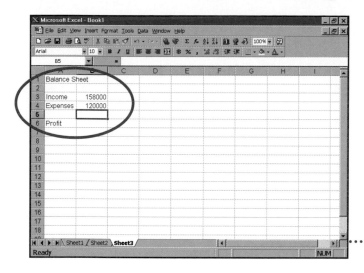

7 To try subtracting, click the **Sheet3** tab to move to Sheet3. Starting in cell A1, type the data that appears in the figure shown here so that your computer screen matches the figure.

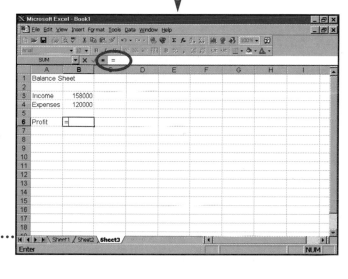

8 Click cell **B6** to place the formula there. (Eventually, Excel will display the result of the formula in this cell.) Type **=**.

9 Select the first cell you want to include in the subtraction formula, in this case cell **B3**. Excel surrounds the cell with a dashed marquee, and =B3 appears in the Formula bar and in cell B6.

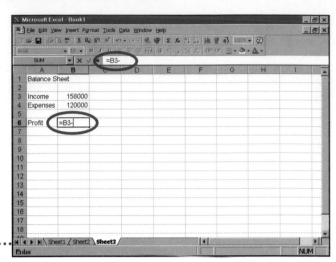

10 Type – to enter the minus sign (–) as the operator. It tells Excel which mathematical operation you want to perform (in this case, subtraction). You now see =B3– in the Formula bar and cell B6. The cell pointer returns to B6.

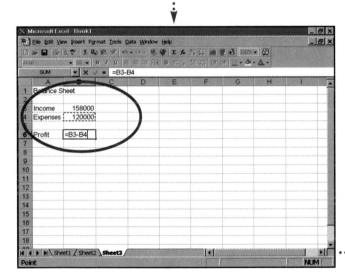

11 Select cell **B4** to make it the second cell in the subtraction formula. A dashed box surrounds the cell, and you see =B3–B4 in the Formula bar and in cell B6.

Puzzled?

If you select the wrong cell, click the **Undo** button on the Standard toolbar.

12 Press **Enter** when you finish creating the formula. You see the result of the formula (38000) in cell B6. Note, however, that anytime cell B6 is the active cell, the formula =B3–B4 appears in the Formula bar. ■

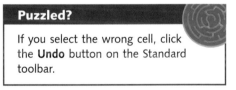
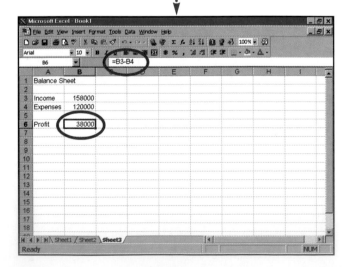

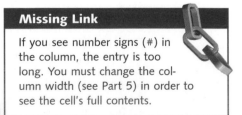

Missing Link

If you see number signs (#) in the column, the entry is too long. You must change the column width (see Part 5) in order to see the cell's full contents.

Multiplying and Dividing Data with a Formula

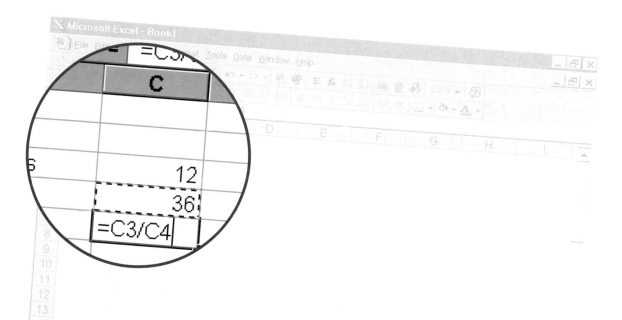

"Why would I do this?"

On an invoice, you might want to calculate the price of each item (each line on the invoice) by multiplying the quantity purchased by the price of a single unit. In a cell that will contain the price, you can just multiply the values in the cells that make up the quantity and unit price (say 20*1.50). (To multiply, press the asterisk (*) key; to divide, press the slash (/) key.) But if you do that and then you change either the quantity or the unit price, the total price becomes inaccurate.

To avoid this, calculate the total price using a formula that references the cells containing the quantity and unit price. When you place such a formula in a cell, Excel updates the cell containing the formula every time you change the value in either of the cells to which the formula refers. That way, if you change the values in either the quantity or unit price cell, the value of the cell containing the total price will remain accurate.

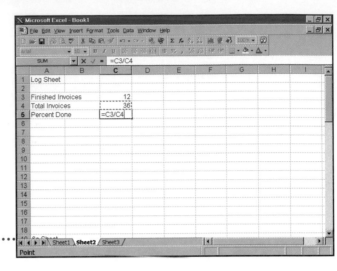

1 Click the **Sheet2** tab to move to Sheet2. Starting in cell A1, type the data that appears in the figure shown here so that your computer screen matches it.

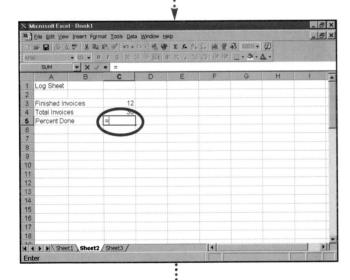

2 Click the cell in which you want to place the formula, in this case cell **C5**. Excel will display the result of the formula there. Type **=**.

Missing Link

Typing an equal sign (=) tells Excel you want to create a formula. You then select the cells you want to include in the formula.

3 Select cell **C3** as the first cell you want to include in the formula. A dashed marquee surrounds the cell, and Excel displays =C3 in the Formula bar and cell C5.

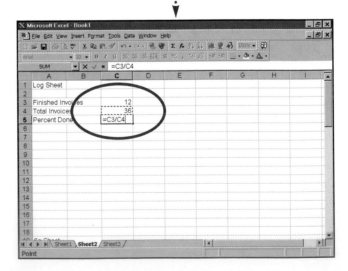

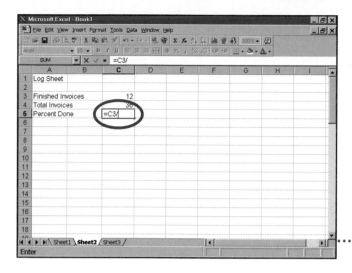

4 Type /. The slash is an operator that tells Excel you want to use the division mathematical operation. The cell pointer returns to C5.

5 Select cell **C4** to have Excel divide the number of Finished Invoices by the Total Invoices. A dashed marquee surrounds the active cell, and Excel displays =C3/C4 in the Formula bar and in cell C5.

Puzzled?

If you make a mistake while entering the division formula, immediately click the **Undo** button in the Standard toolbar to delete the most recent entry.

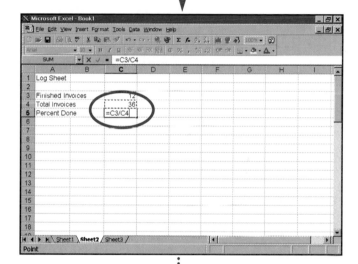

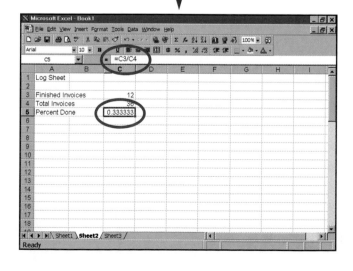

6 Press **Enter** to enter the formula. The result of the formula (0.333333) appears in cell C5. However, anytime C5 is the active cell, =C3/C4 appears in the Formula bar. ■

Missing Link

If you see number signs (#) in the column, the entry is too large to fit in the column. You must change the column width (see Part 5) to view all of the cell's contents.

91

TASK

26

Totaling Cells with the SUM Function

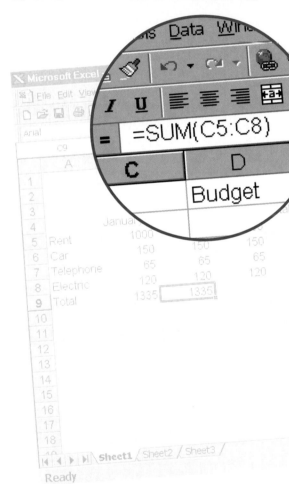

=SUM(C5:C8)

"Why would I do this?"

A *function* is a predefined formula. To use a function, you provide the variable parts of the formula, and Excel calculates the result. For example, using the SUM function, you can add the numbers that appear in a range of cells without having to type each cell address and type the plus sign over and over. And if you later insert or delete rows (or columns), Excel automatically updates the total.

Because adding many rows or columns of numbers is such a common activity, Excel includes the AutoSum button on the Standard toolbar to make entering the function easier.

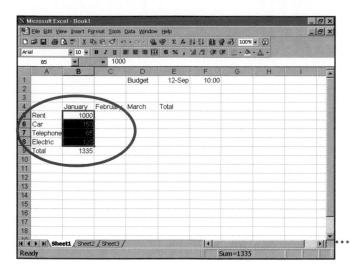

1 Click the **Sheet1** tab to move to the budget on Sheet1. Then select the range B5:B8 by selecting cell **B5** and dragging the mouse down to cell **B8**. B5:B8 is the range that contains the numbers you will use to fill columns C and D.

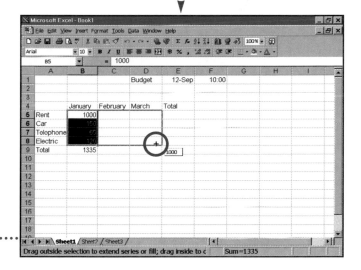

2 Move the mouse pointer to the fill handle in the lower-right corner of cell B8 until the mouse pointer changes to a black plus sign. Then drag the selected range to the right, across columns C and D. Excel fills the range C5:D8 with the numbers from column B.

3 Click cell **C9**, which is where you will place the SUM function.

4 Double-click the **AutoSum** button on the Standard toolbar to enter the SUM function in the Formula bar and in the selected cell. Excel displays =SUM(C5:C8) in the Formula bar and displays the result of the formula, 1335, in cell C9.

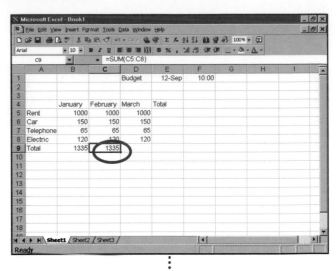

Missing Link

If you single-click the AutoSum button, you see the formula in cell C9 before Excel places its result in the cell. Double-clicking accepts the formula.

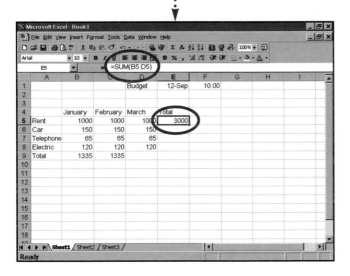

5 To sum the values in a row, click in cell **E5** and double-click the **AutoSum** button. The formula =SUM(B5:D5) appears in the Formula bar, and the result of the formula, 3000, appears in cell E5. ■

Puzzled?

If you prefer to use the keyboard, you can press **Alt** + = to create a SUM formula. Then press **Enter** to place the formula in the active cell.

Calculating an Average

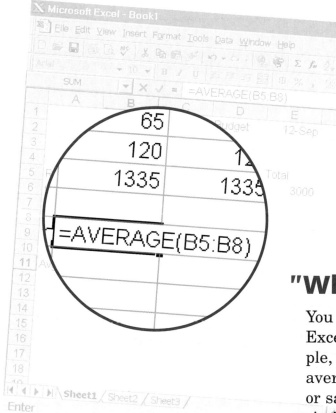

"Why would I do this?"

You can calculate an average by using Excel's AVERAGE function. For example, you might want to calculate an average expense, income, grade, rating, or salary. The AVERAGE function is similar to the SUM function: it totals the values in a range of cells and divides that total by the number of cells. And all you have to do is select the range of cells and tell it to go to work!

For this example, you'll work in the Budget sheet and find the average of the total expenses for January. You will enter the label Avg Expense in cell A11 and use the AVERAGE function in cell B11.

Task 27: Calculating an Average

1 Click cell **A11**, type **Avg Expense**, and press the right-arrow key. The cell pointer moves to cell B11, which is where you want to place the formula that calculates an average.

Missing Link

Notice that the long label in cell A11 spills into cell B11. You can widen column A to accommodate the long entry. See Task 46, "Changing Column Width and Row Height," for details.

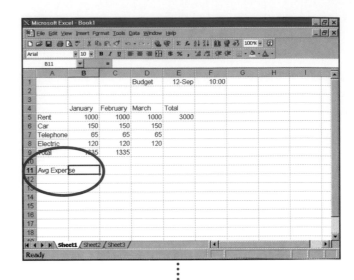

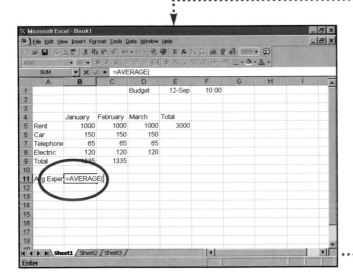

2 Type **=AVERAGE(**. You can type the function in lowercase or uppercase letters. You enter the range that you want to average within the parentheses.

3 Drag over cells **B5**, **B6**, **B7**, and **B8** to select them (the range is B5:B8). In the Formula bar and in cell B11, Excel displays =AVERAGE(B5:B8. A marquee surrounds the selected range.

Missing Link

The ScreenTip that appears as you drag tells you the number of rows and columns you have selected.

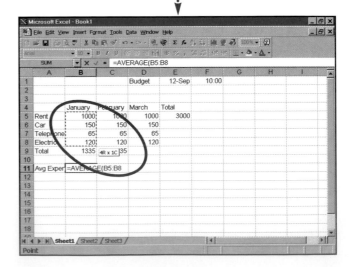

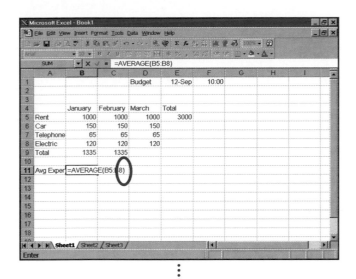

4 Type **)** to tell Excel that you are finished selecting the range. Excel inserts the range in the parentheses. In the Formula bar and cell B11, you see =AVERAGE(B5:B8).

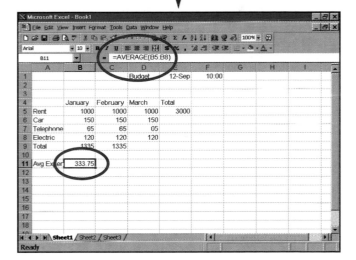

5 Press **Enter** to confirm the formula. Excel displays the result of the function (333.75) in cell B11. If you highlight cell B11 again, you see the formula it contains in the Formula bar. ■

Puzzled?

To delete the most recent entry, click the **Undo** button in the Standard toolbar immediately after entering the AVERAGE function.

TASK 28

Using AutoCalculate

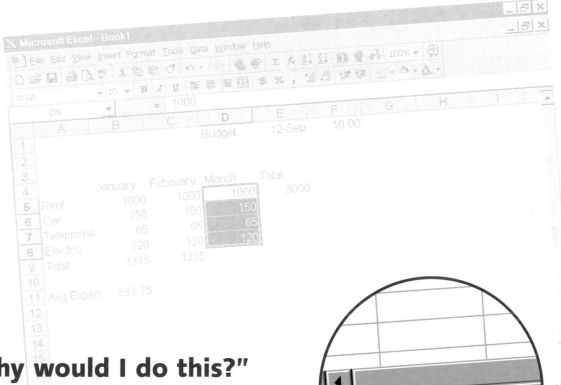

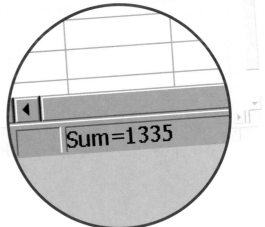

"Why would I do this?"

Many times when you're working in a worksheet, you will want to know the sum of a group of numbers but you won't need to save that sum. In other words, you want to create a SUM function, but you don't really want to include it in the worksheet.

You can use the AutoCalculate feature of Excel to get a quick sum, average, or count of values without actually entering a function into a cell.

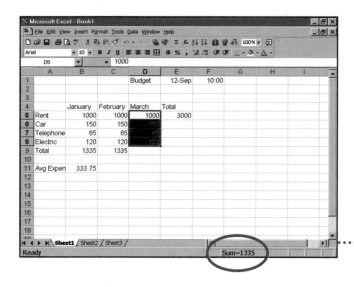

1 In the Budget worksheet, select cells **D5:D8**. Toward the right end of the status bar, you'll see that Excel has added the selected range and displays the result.

2 To see the average or the count of the selected range, move the mouse pointer into the status bar and click the right mouse button to access a shortcut menu.

Missing Link

Use the COUNT function in Excel to get a count of the number of cells in a specified range that contain numeric values. For example, this function might be useful if you wanted to count the number of students in a class that you listed in a worksheet.

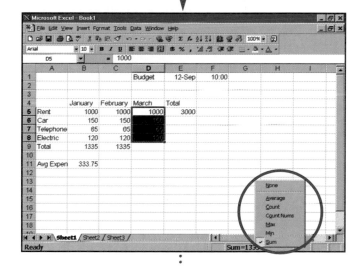

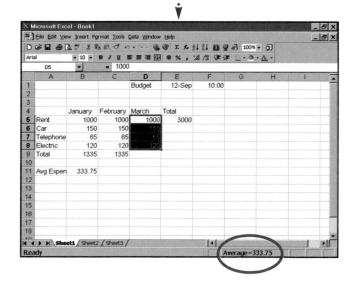

3 Select the appropriate choice from the shortcut menu. For example, select **Average**, and the average appears in the status bar where the sum used to be. ■

Using the Paste Function

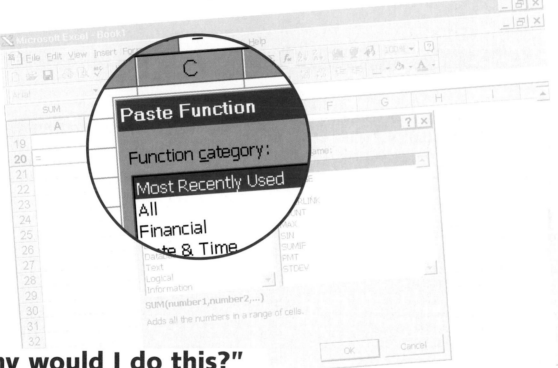

"Why would I do this?"

What do you do when you want to try a function but you don't know how to set it up? Use Excel's future value function and let the Paste Function button on the Standard toolbar help you set up the function.

For example, suppose you want to save money for a special birthday present. You start by depositing $50 into a savings account that earns 6 percent annual interest compounded monthly

(monthly interest of 6 percent/12, or 0.5 percent per month). In addition, you plan to deposit $5 at the beginning of every month for the next 12 months. How much money will be in the account at the end of 12 months? (Don't you just HATE story problems?) You might not know which calculations to perform to get an answer, but if you can plug in values for the variables, Excel can find the answer for you.

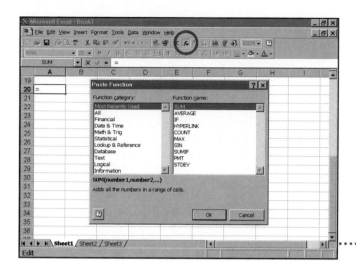

1 Click cell **A20** of the Budget worksheet to select it, and then click the **Paste Function** button on the Standard toolbar.

2 In the Paste Function dialog box, click **Financial** in the Function Category list on the left. Then click **FV** in the Function Name list on the right.

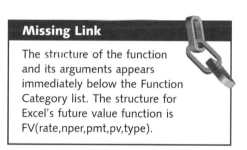

Missing Link

The structure of the function and its arguments appears immediately below the Function Category list. The structure for Excel's future value function is FV(rate,nper,pmt,pv,type).

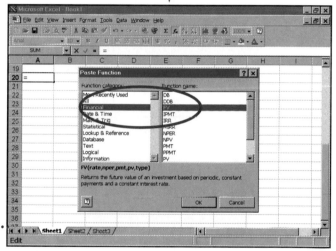

3 Click **OK**, and Excel displays a new box, into which you are prompted to enter values for each argument of the function you selected—in this case, the FV function.

Puzzled?

Although this box doesn't look like a traditional dialog box (it has no title bar), you can move it around on-screen by dragging. Point the mouse at any gray area of the box and then drag. (For this figure, I moved the box so that you could see the formula being built in cell A20.)

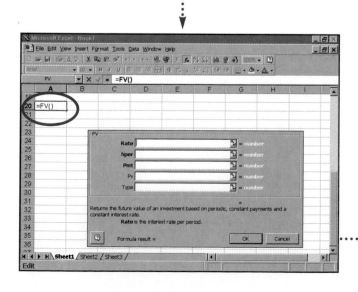

4 For the Rate, you enter the rate per period. Because 6 percent annually is .5 percent monthly, you would enter the decimal equivalent of .5 percent. Type **.005**. You can also enter **.5%**, or even the formula **6%/12**, and Excel will convert the value to .005.

Puzzled?

As you type a value, Excel tries to calculate the value of the function "so far." In the lower-left corner of the dialog box (next to the Help button), you can see Excel calculating the function's value using the information provided.

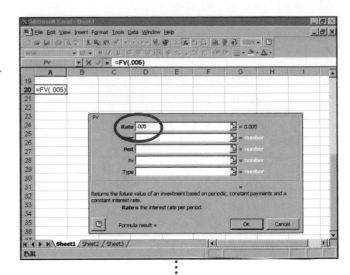

5 Nper represents the total number of payments you intend to make while you save. Because you will make monthly deposits for one year, enter 12.

Missing Link

If you want to move between text boxes using the keyboard, press the **Tab** key. Pressing the Enter key is the same as clicking the OK button.

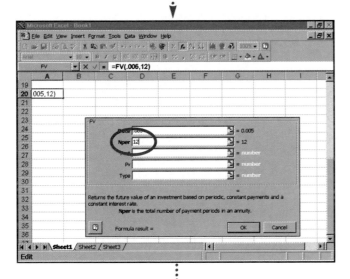

6 For Pmt, enter the amount of money you intend to deposit each month. For example, type **–5**.

Puzzled?

For the FV and PV functions, all money that you put out (such as payments and initial deposits) should be entered as a negative value. Think of this as "outflow" from your pocket.

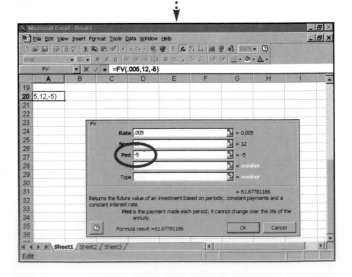

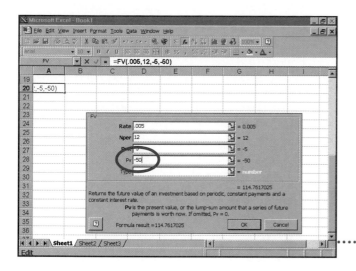

7 Pv is optional and represents the amount of money you initially deposit. For this example, type **-50**.

8 Use the Type box to tell Excel if you are making payments at the beginning or end of the period. Enter 0 for payments made at the end of the period or 1 for payments made at the beginning of the period. For this example, type **1**.

Missing Link

The timing of the payment affects the amount of interest that will accrue.

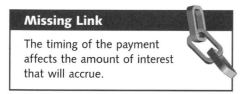

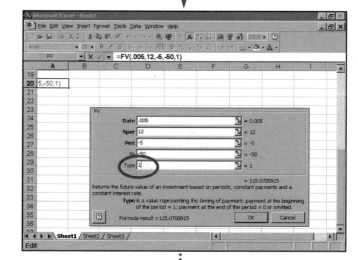

9 Click **OK**, and Excel displays the result of the function in the selected cell. As you can see, if you carried out this example, you would have $115.07 after a year. ■

Puzzled?

The result of the function may be too large to fit in the column. If you see number signs (#) in the cell, make the column wider. (See Task 46, "Changing Column Width and Row Height" for help.)

Calculating a Conditional Sum

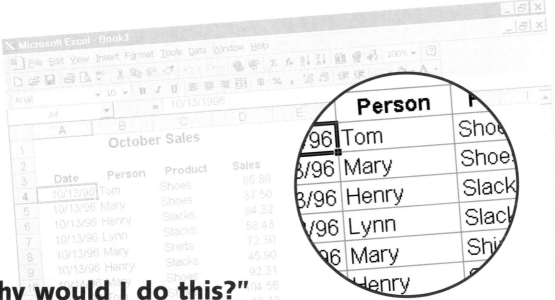

"Why would I do this?"

Suppose you only want to display a sum for a column of numbers if it meets some criteria. With the Conditional Sum Wizard, you can tell Excel to sum only the numbers that meet the criteria you specify. Suppose, for example, that your company pays your sales force a commission based on the salesperson's total sales over a month. Further, suppose that your sales force of four people sells a variety of products, and the records you get are each day's receipts. Because a receipt could contain multiple

products, calculating total sales for each salesperson could be a *very* time-consuming job. If, however, you enter the contents of each receipt so that one line on the receipt appears in one row in Excel, you can use the Conditional Sum Wizard to easily calculate the total sales for each person.

The Conditional Sum Wizard is an add-in program that you must install. If you don't see it when you try these steps, rerun the installation program and install the Conditional Sum Wizard add-in program.

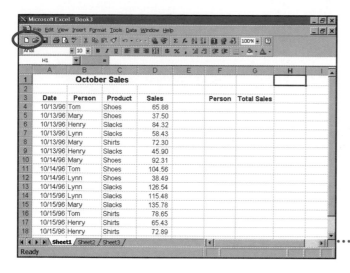

1 Click the **New** button on the Standard toolbar and set up a worksheet that looks like the one shown here.

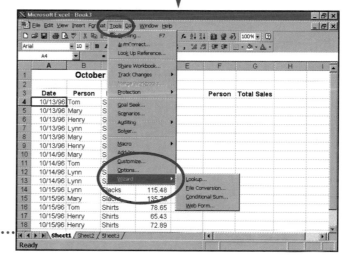

2 Click any cell containing information. Then open the **Tools** menu and highlight the **Wizard** command.

3 From the submenu that appears, choose **Conditional Sum**. Excel displays the first Conditional Sum Wizard dialog box.

Missing Link

Notice that Excel places a flashing marquee in the background around the range it thinks you want to sum, including the column labels. The range you want to sum must include the column labels.

4 If Excel selected the range and labels correctly, click the **Next** button. Excel displays the second wizard dialog box.

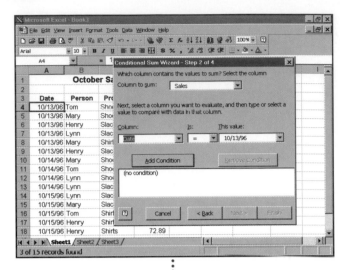

Missing Link

If Excel selected the wrong range, click the **Collapse Dialog** button (at the right edge of the range text box) to shrink the dialog box to just its title bar. In the worksheet, select the correct range you want to use, and then click the **Expand Dialog** button to redisplay the full dialog box.

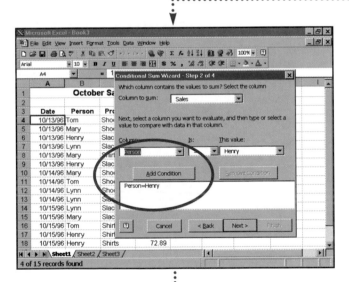

5 Set the conditions you want Excel to use when summing. In this example, Excel guessed correctly that we want to sum the **Sales** column. To set the conditions, choose **Person** from the **Column** list box, leave the **Is** list box set at **=**, and select a person's name (such as Henry) from the **This Value** list box. Click the **Add Condition** button, and the condition appears at the bottom of the dialog box.

6 Click **Next**. From the third Conditional Sum Wizard, choose whether you want Excel to copy just the formula into your worksheet or the formula and the conditional values. For this example, choose the formula and the conditional values.

Puzzled?

Copying the formula and the conditional values is particularly useful if your conditional values change frequently; for example, if your sales force changes frequently.

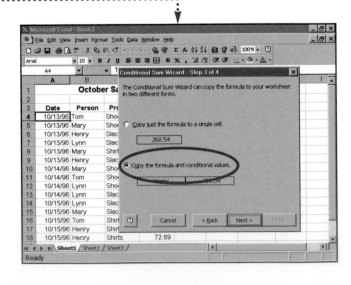

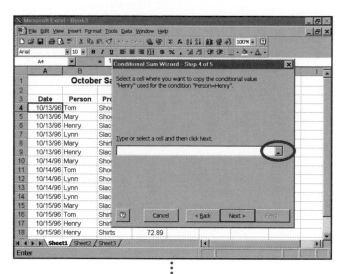

7 Click **Next**. To select a cell where you want the conditional value to appear, use the **Collapse Dialog** button to shrink the dialog box and move it out of the way.

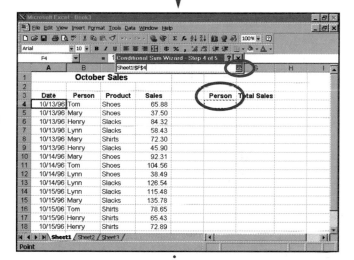

8 Select the cell where you want the conditional value. For this example, click cell **F4** to place the salesperson's name there. Then click the **Expand Dialog** button to redisplay the Conditional Sum Wizard.

9 Click **Next**. To select a cell where you want the conditional sum to appear, use the **Collapse Dialog** button to shrink the dialog box and move it out of the way.

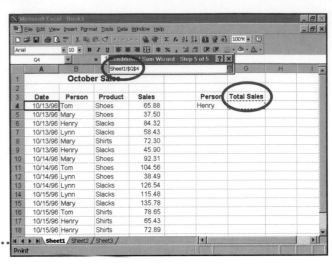

10 Select the cell where you want the conditional sum. For this example, click cell **G4** to place the salesperson's sales results there.

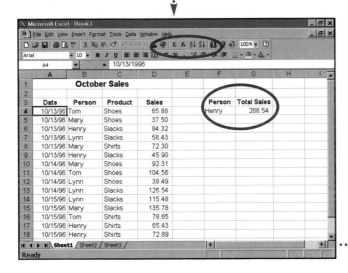

11 Click the **Expand Dialog** button to redisplay the Conditional Sum Wizard and then click **Finish**. Excel displays your worksheet and shows you the result—such as Henry's total sales.

12 Repeat these steps to calculate additional conditional sums. For example, sum Tom's, Mary's, and Lynn's sales results. ■

Missing Link

You can also create conditional sums to get total sales for each product or total sales by date. You would change the conditions you set in step 5 to use Products or Dates.

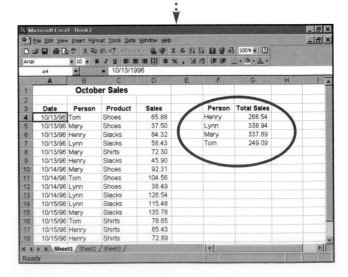

Copying a Formula

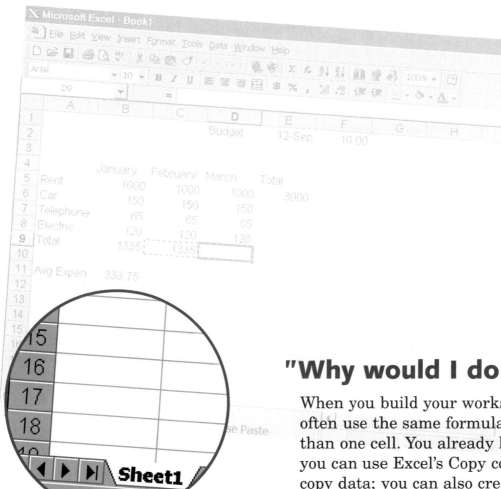

"Why would I do this?"

When you build your worksheet, you often use the same formulas in more than one cell. You already learned that you can use Excel's Copy command to copy data; you can also create a formula once and then copy that formula to other appropriate cells. This saves you from having to go to each cell and enter the same basic formula. For example, you might want to copy a formula across a totals row so that you won't have to type a formula to add up each row of numbers.

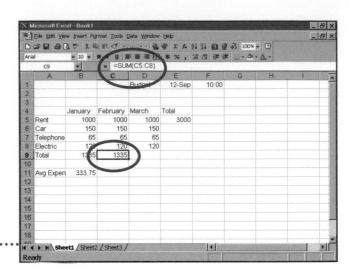

1 In the Budget worksheet, click cell **C9**, which contains the formula to add the numbers in C5:C8.

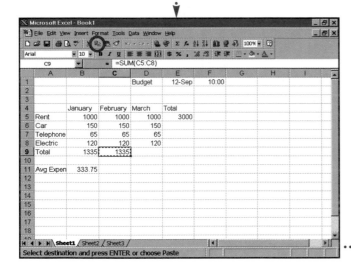

2 Click the **Copy** button on the Standard toolbar. A dashed marquee surrounds C9, the cell you are copying. The message Select destination and press ENTER or choose Paste appears in the status bar to remind you how to complete the task.

3 Click cell **D9** so you can copy the formula from cell C9 into it. (When you copy the formula, it will adapt to its surroundings, changing the range from C5:C8 to D5:D8.)

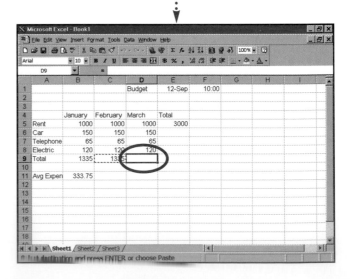

Missing Link

The formula in C9 uses *relative addressing*. That means that when you copy the formula, Excel automatically adjusts the cell references to reflect the new location. If you use *absolute addressing* it won't change the formula.

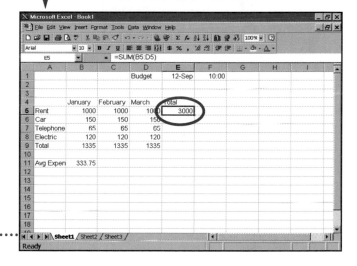

4 Click the **Paste** button on the Standard toolbar to paste a copy of the formula from cell C9 into cell D9. Then press **Esc** to remove the dashed marquee. The result of the formula appears in cell D9, and the formula appears in the Formula bar.

Missing Link

In this step, you can just press **Enter.** You click Paste if you want to copy the formula to more than one location. As long as the marquee remains around the original cell, you can Paste the formula in as many locations as you want.

5 To use the "drag-and-drop" method, copy the formula in cell E5 to cells E6:E9. First, click cell **E5** to select the cell that contains the formula you want to copy.

6 Move the mouse pointer to the fill handle in the lower-right corner of cell E5 until the mouse pointer changes to a large black plus sign. Then drag downward across cells **E6**, **E7**, **E8**, and **E9**. When you release the mouse button, Excel fills the range E6:E9 with the formula from cell E5. Click any cell to remove the highlight. (You might find it interesting to click cell **E6** and examine the formula in the Formula bar.) ■

TASK 32

Naming a Range

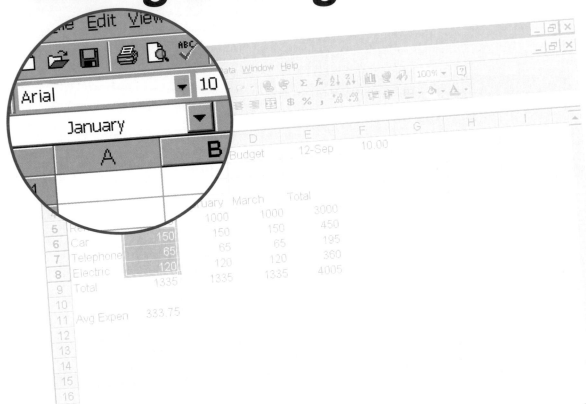

"Why would I do this?"

Naming ranges offers several advantages. Names are easier to remember than cell addresses are. And you can use range names in formulas. For example, suppose you use the SUM function to add a column of values, and the formula reads =SUM(B5:B8). If you were to name the range B5:B8 "JANUARY," you could add that column with the function =SUM(JANUARY). Names

must start with a letter or underscore, and a range name can contain 255 characters.

If you have created many named ranges, you may want to make a list that tells you the name of each range and its cell addresses. After you name some ranges in the Budget worksheet, use Excel's Paste Name dialog box to create such a list.

1 Select cells **B5**, **B6**, **B7**, and **B8**, which make up the range you want to name (B5:B8).

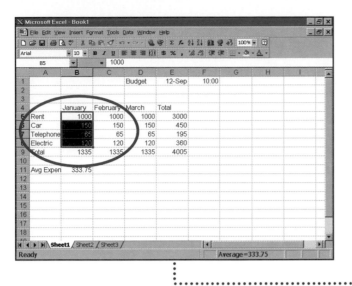

Missing Link

You must start names with a letter, and you can use lower-case or uppercase letters. However, you can't use spaces, and you should not use a name that looks like a cell address (B15, for example).

2 Click the drop-down arrow beside the Name box in the Formula bar. Excel opens the list box, highlights the cell address B5, and moves it to the left side of the Name box.

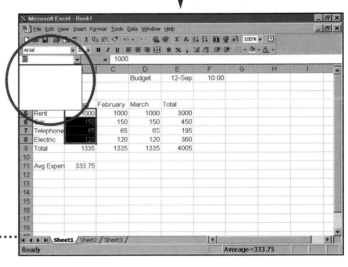

3 Type the name you want to assign to the range. In this case, type **January**. Then press **Enter** to confirm the range name you want to assign, and Excel adds the range name to the list of names in the Name box. (It assigns "January" to cells B5 through B8.)

4 Repeat steps 1–3 to assign the name **February** to the range C5:C8 and to assign **March** to range D5:D8.

Missing Link

Excel saves the name with the workbook when you save the workbook. Then when you select the range, the range name appears in the Name box in the Formula bar.

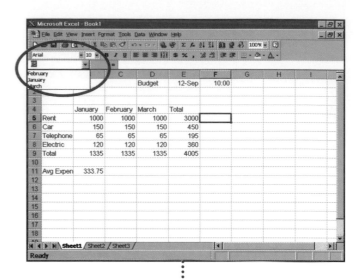

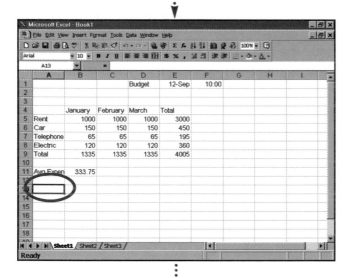

5 To create a list of named ranges in the worksheet, first click cell **A13**. The list of range names will start in cell A13.

Missing Link

The list of names is two columns wide and as many rows long as there are names. Be sure to place the table of names in a location where it won't overwrite any data.

6 Click **Insert** in the menu bar, select **Name**, and choose **Paste**. Excel opens the Paste Name dialog box.

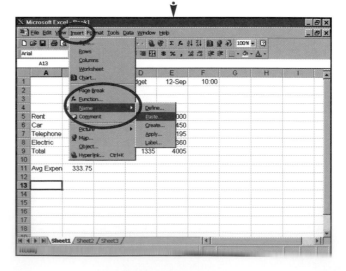

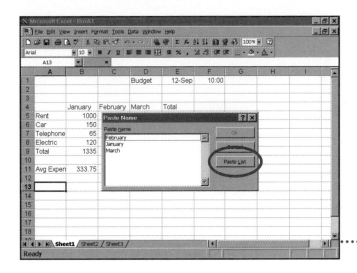

7 Click the **Paste List** button to paste the list into your worksheet in the location of the cell pointer.

8 Click any cell to deselect the range, and Excel inserts the two-column table in a range beginning with cell A13. The first column lists the range names in alphabetical order; the second column lists the range coordinates for each name. ■

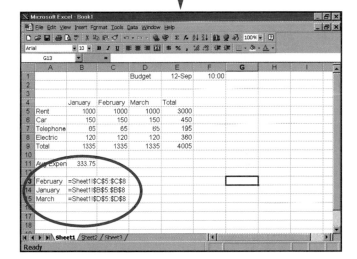

Puzzled?

To delete a range name, select the **Insert**, **Name**, **Define** command, select the name in the **Names in Workbook** list box, and click **Delete**. Then click **OK**.

PART
IV

Managing
Workbooks

▲ ● ■ ▲ ● ■ ▲ ●

T'S TIME TO LEARN ABOUT managing workbook files in Excel. In this part, you learn how to save your work, abandon a workbook that you don't want to save, create a new workbook, open a workbook, find a workbook, close a workbook, and rename the sheets in a workbook. You might already be familiar with using windows inside applications such as Excel. If you want to skip the first part of this section, feel free to do so, but be sure to read the tasks on how to find a workbook and rename sheets within a workbook.

Unless you loaded a special *add-in* (a small optional program that you can install when you install Excel), Excel does not automatically save your work, so you should save every five or ten minutes. If you don't save your work, you could lose it. Suppose that you have been working on a worksheet for a few hours and your power goes off unexpectedly—an air-conditioning repairman at your office shorts out the power, or a thunderstorm hits, or something else causes a power loss. If you haven't saved, you lose all of your hard work.

Saving a file that you previously saved is slightly different from saving a newly created workbook. When you save a workbook you saved before, you save the current version on-screen and overwrite the original version on disk. This means you always have the most current version of your file stored on disk.

If you want to keep both versions—the on-screen version and the original—you can use the File, Save As command to save the on-screen version with a different name. Saving a file with a new name gives you two copies of the same worksheet with differences in their data. When you save a file with a new name, you also can save the file in a different directory or drive.

Saving a workbook does not remove it from the screen. To remove a workbook from the screen, you must close the workbook. Whether you've saved a workbook or not, you can close it using the File, Close command.

You can open more than one workbook at a time. For example, you might have two separate workbooks that contain related information. While using one workbook, you can view the information in another, or even copy information from one workbook to the other. The number of workbooks you can open depends on the amount of memory available in your computer.

When you open and view several workbooks, they might overlap—essentially hiding workbooks beneath other workbooks. Excel lets you rearrange the workbooks in several different ways so that some part of each workbook is visible. Arranging windows so that you can see some small part of each window is handy when you want to compare the figures in two workbooks side by side. You can use the Arrange command on the Window menu to arrange the windows. If you want to display one workbook after you are finished using the multiple window arrangement, you can close the other workbooks (or you can leave them open) and simply maximize the window you want to use. The workbook you want to display fills the screen.

Sometimes you simply forget where you stored certain information. Excel lets you search for a workbook using any search criteria such as the file name, disk, or folder location.

As you learned earlier, a new Excel workbook has three sheets by default and can contain as many as 255 sheets (depending on your computer's available memory). The sheets are named Sheet1 through Sheet3. You can rename sheets to clearly identify the contents of each sheet. For example, you can rename Sheet1 to QTR 1, rename Sheet2 to QTR 2, and so on. You also can add worksheets to and delete worksheets from a workbook.

Saving a Workbook

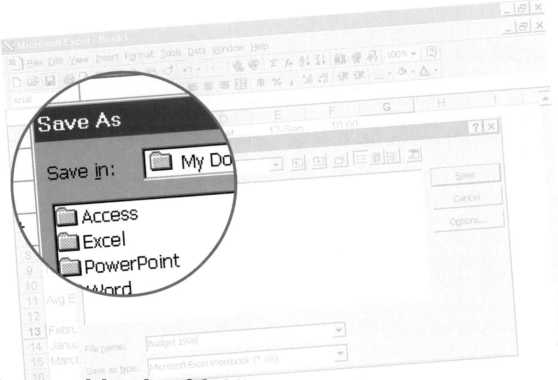

"Why would I do this?"

Until you save the workbook, your data is not stored on a disk. You can lose your data if something happens, such as a power loss. Once you save a workbook, you can retrieve it from the disk when you need the workbook again. You should save your work every five or ten minutes and at the end of a work session. Then close the workbook if you want to clear the screen.

When naming a file, you don't need to worry about an extension; by default, Excel will save your workbook as an Excel file and assign the extension automatically for you. And because of Windows 95's "long names" capability, you are no longer limited to eight characters, and file names can include spaces. However, file names cannot include the following characters: / \ > < * ? " | : ;.

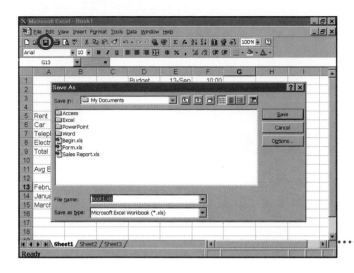

1 Click the **Save** button on the Standard toolbar to select the Save command located on the File menu. The first time you save the workbook, Excel displays the Save As dialog box.

2 Type a name for your workbook in the **File Name** text box. For example, type **Budget 1996**. If you see the folder in which you want to store your workbook, double-click it. If you don't see it, open the **Save In** list box and navigate to the folder in which you want to store your workbook.

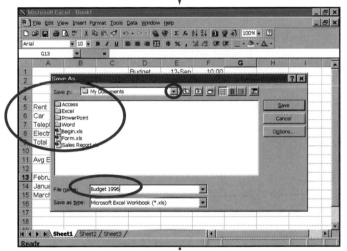

Missing Link

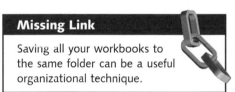

Saving all your workbooks to the same folder can be a useful organizational technique.

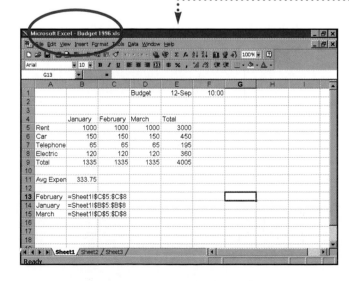

3 Click **Save**, and Excel redisplays the workbook. The workbook's new name, Budget 1996.xls, appears in the title bar. ∎

Puzzled?

If you type a file name that already exists, Excel displays an alert box that asks Replace existing file?. Click **Cancel** to return to the Save As dialog box, and then type a new name.

Closing a Workbook

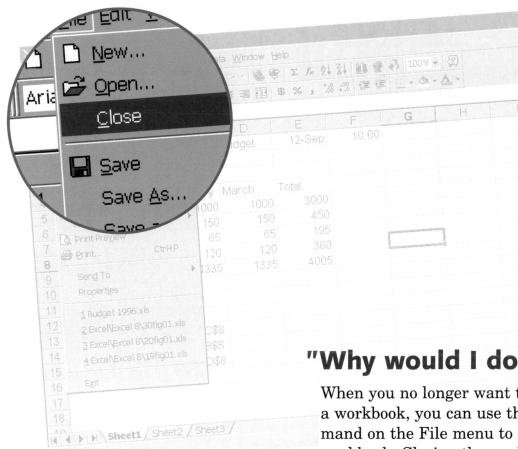

"Why would I do this?"

When you no longer want to work with a workbook, you can use the Close command on the File menu to close the workbook. Closing the workbook removes it from your screen, but as long as you save the workbook it will be available on disk.

You can use the Open button on the Standard toolbar to reopen a closed workbook. If you want to start a new workbook, use the New Workbook button on the Standard toolbar.

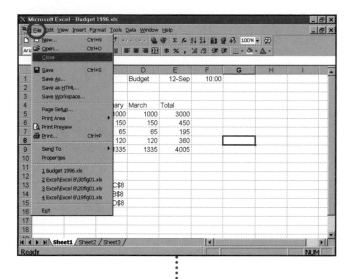

1 Click **File** in the menu bar. Excel opens the File menu.

Missing Link

You can also click the **Close** (X) button in the upper-right corner of the workbook window to close a workbook. Make sure you click the Close button of the lower set of three icons—the one for the workbook window. The upper Close box closes the program, not just the workbook.

2 Click the **Close** command. If you saved the file immediately before choosing the File, Close command, Excel closes the workbook. You see just the toolbars and menu bar. From here, you can open a workbook or create a new workbook.

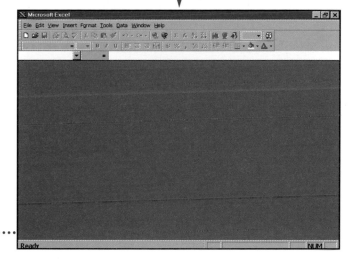

3 If you made changes, Excel displays an alert box that reminds you to save your changes. Click **Yes** to save the changes and close the workbook. If you made changes you don't want to save, choose **No** to ignore the changes and close the workbook. ■

Puzzled?

If you need to make more changes before closing, click **Cancel**, and Excel takes you back to the workbook.

Creating a New Workbook

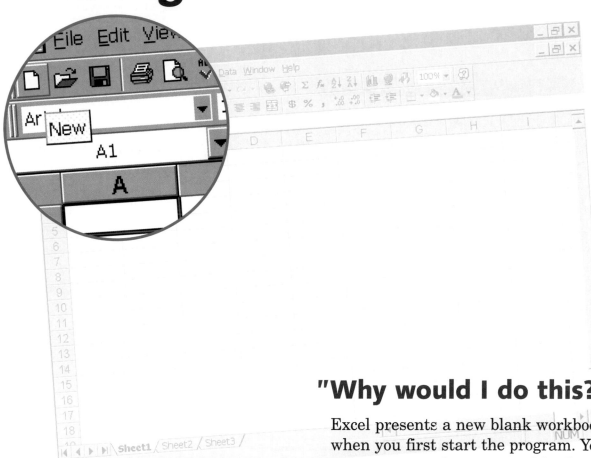

"Why would I do this?"

Excel presents a new blank workbook when you first start the program. You can create another new workbook at any time. You might do this if, perhaps, you have closed and saved the active workbook and want to begin a new one. Or you might want to create a new workbook and still keep the existing one open (if you want to copy text from the original one to the new one, for example).

In this task, you'll create a new workbook and see how it works. Then you'll close the new workbook.

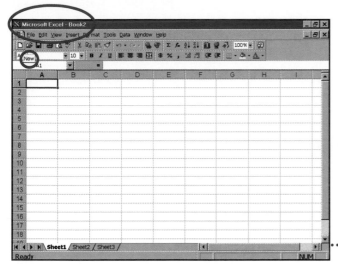

1 Click the **New** button on the Standard toolbar. Clicking the New button selects the File, New command. A blank workbook appears on-screen with the title **Book2**. (The number varies depending on the number of workbooks you have opened during a session.)

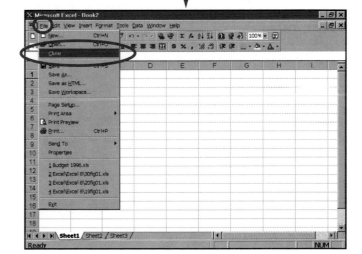

2 Click **File** in the menu bar and select **Close** to abandon the new workbook. Excel closes the workbook. ■

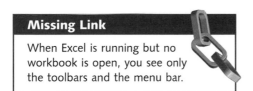

Missing Link

When Excel is running but no workbook is open, you see only the toolbars and the menu bar.

Opening a Workbook

"Why would I do this?"

After you save and close a workbook, you can open it again to make changes to it. Or perhaps you want to examine the sample workbooks that came with Excel. The sample workbooks are stored in Excel's EXAMPLES folder.

1 Suppose you want to work with the Budget 1996 file again. Click the **Open** button on the Standard toolbar to select the File, Open command. Excel displays the Open dialog box.

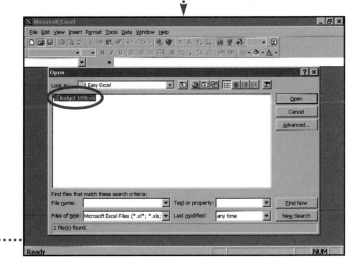

Missing Link

The Open dialog box also contains the Look In list. If the workbook doesn't appear in the window, open the **Look In** list box and select the folder that contains the workbook.

2 Highlight the file you want to open. For example, highlight **Budget 1996.xls**.

3 Click the **Open** button. Excel opens the workbook and displays it on-screen. The file name appears in the title bar. (You can also open a file by double-clicking the file name.) ■

Puzzled?

If you loaded wallpapers when you loaded Windows 95, your Desktop background may look different than what you see in the figures in this task.

Finding a Workbook

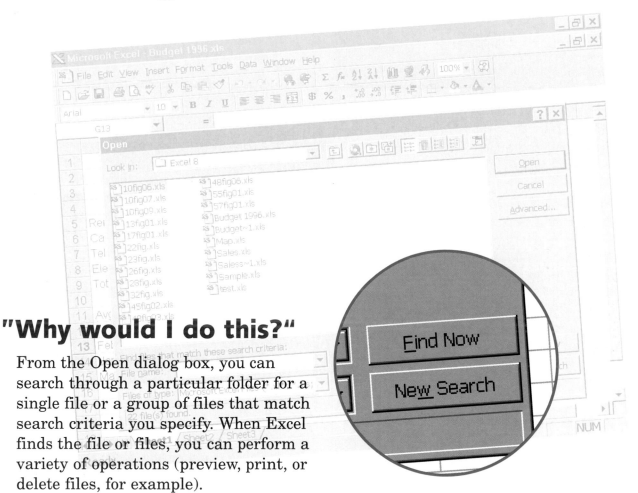

"Why would I do this?"

From the Open dialog box, you can search through a particular folder for a single file or a group of files that match search criteria you specify. When Excel finds the file or files, you can perform a variety of operations (preview, print, or delete files, for example).

Searching this way comes in handy when you can't remember the name of a file that contains certain information. For instance, if you're looking for the file that contains your January budget, you could search for all files containing the word January.

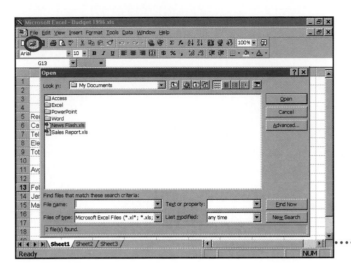

1 Click the **Open** button on the Standard toolbar to select the File, Open command. Excel displays the Open dialog box.

2 Move to the folder you want to search by clicking the arrow next to the Look In list box or by double-clicking a folder in the box below the Look In list box.

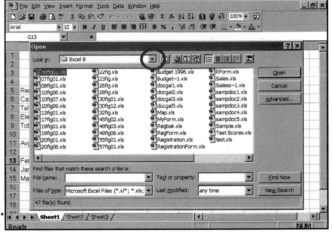

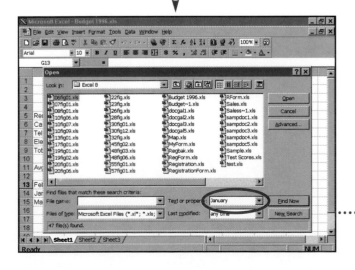

3 Click in the **Text or Property** box and type **January** (or whatever text you want to search for). By default, Excel searches all Excel files (as indicated in the Files of Type text box). However, you can search other file types.

Missing Link

By clicking the Advanced button, you can specify advanced search criteria, and you can save search criteria.

4 Click the **Find Now** button. Excel searches the contents of the files in the current folder for the word January and displays in the list only those that meet the search criteria.

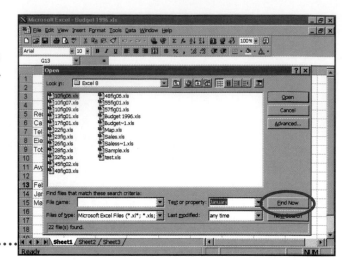

Puzzled?

To redisplay all the files in the folder, remove the search criteria and click the **Find Now** button again.

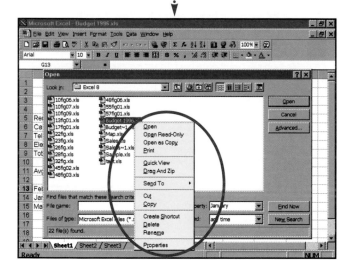

5 To open, print, or delete a file that met the search criteria, highlight the file, right-click it, and select your choice from the shortcut menu. ■

Missing Link

To preview a file's contents, click the **Preview** button (the second button from the right end at the top of the Open dialog box).

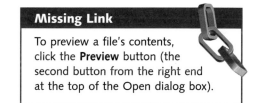

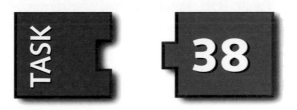
Renaming, Adding, Moving, and Deleting Sheets

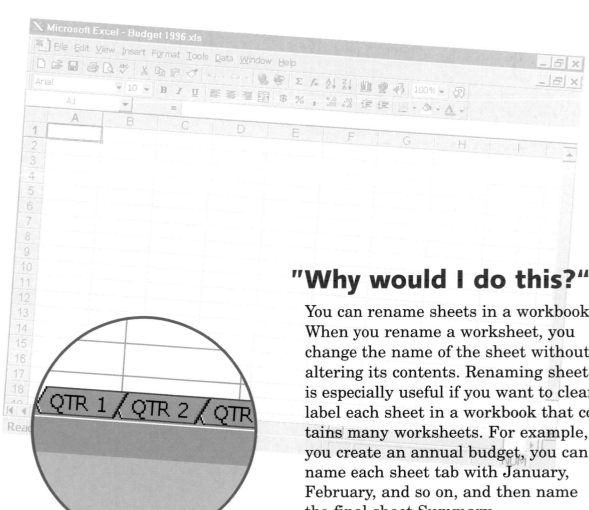

"Why would I do this?"

You can rename sheets in a workbook. When you rename a worksheet, you change the name of the sheet without altering its contents. Renaming sheets is especially useful if you want to clearly label each sheet in a workbook that contains many worksheets. For example, if you create an annual budget, you can name each sheet tab with January, February, and so on, and then name the final sheet Summary.

In addition to renaming sheets, you also can add sheets to and delete sheets from a workbook.

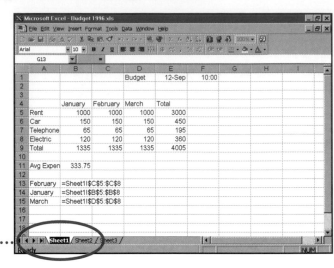

1 Double-click the **Sheet1** tab. Excel highlights the name of the Sheet tab.

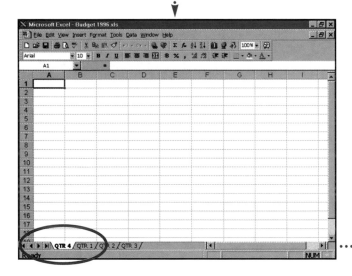

2 Type the name you want to give the sheet, such as **QTR 1**. As a rule, you can use no more than 31 characters, including spaces. Press **Enter** to rename the sheet.

3 Repeat steps 1 and 2 to rename **Sheet2** with the name **QTR 2** and to rename **Sheet3** with the name **QTR 3**.

Puzzled?

If you rename the wrong tab, just repeat the procedure using the tab's original name. Then start over with the process of renaming the correct tab.

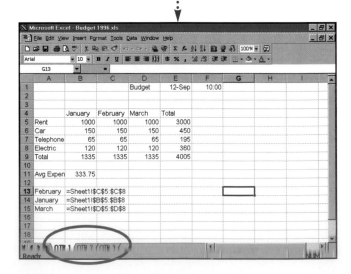

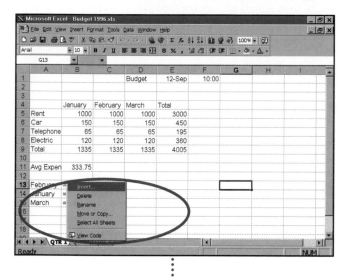

4 To add a sheet for the fourth quarter's data, right-click the sheet tab for **QTR1**. Excel displays a shortcut menu.

Missing Link

Excel adds new sheets in front of the selected sheet. Therefore, you can never add a sheet at the end of the workbook; you must add a sheet and move it to the end of the workbook.

5 Choose **Insert**. Excel displays the insert dialog box, in which you choose what you want to insert.

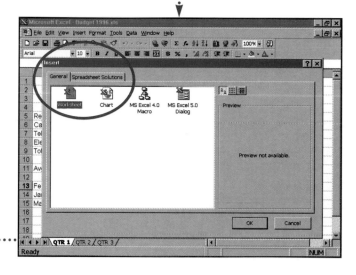

6 Click the **Worksheet** icon and click **OK**. Excel inserts the new sheet (Sheet2) in front of QTR 1.

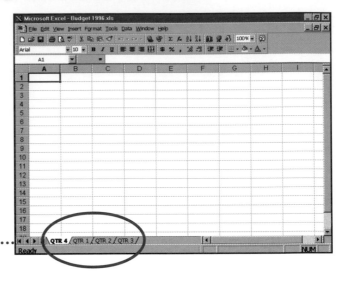

7 Rename Sheet1 as **QTR 4**.

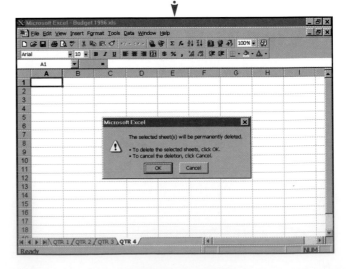

8 To move QTR 4 to its correct location, drag the sheet tab. As you drag, you'll notice a small black arrow that indicates where the sheet would appear if you quit dragging.

9 To delete a sheet, right-click its tab and choose **Delete** from the shortcut menu. Excel displays the confirmation dialog box shown here. Click **OK** (or click **Cancel** to keep the sheet). ■

Puzzled?

You can't undo the deletion of a sheet, so make sure you no longer need the data. And don't forget that other sheets may contain formulas that depend on data appearing on the sheet you want to delete.

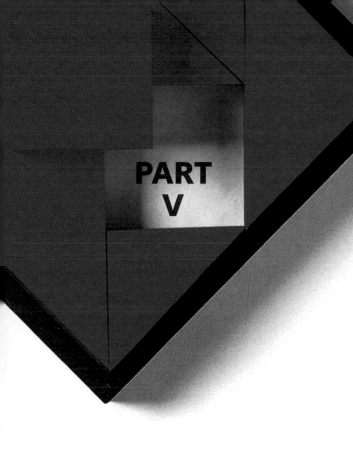

PART V

Formatting the Worksheet

▲ ● ■ ■ ▲ ● ● ■ ▲ ●

YOU CAN CHANGE THE APPEARANCE AND LAYOUT of data on your worksheet through formatting. With Excel's formatting tools, you can make your worksheet more attractive and readable. In this part, you first learn how to automatically format ranges in your worksheet. Then if you prefer to exercise greater control over the appearance of the worksheet, you can use the techniques for centering and right-aligning data in a cell, displaying dollar signs, commas, and percent signs, for changing the number of decimal places, and for formatting a date and a time. You also learn how to copy formats with Excel's Format Painter button, change column width and row height, merge cells in rows or columns, format individual words, add cell comments, shade cells, add borders, and turn off gridlines.

You can align data in a cell to the left, center, or right. The default alignment is General. *General alignment* means that numbers, dates, and times are right-aligned, and text is left-aligned.

There will be many times you will format cells that don't have numbers in them yet. For example, in your workbook, on the Qtr 2 sheet, the cells contain the values for Rent, Food, Telephone, Car, and Total for the second quarter. You can format those cells with commas even though the cells don't contain numbers yet. Then when you do enter numbers into those cells, they automatically appear with commas.

Excel lets you change the width of any column and the height of any row. You can use the AutoFit feature to quickly change the width of any column or the height of any row. Just double-click the line next to the right of the column letter or below the row number of the column or row you want to adjust. Excel automatically changes the width of the column or the height of the row based on the longest entry in that column. If you want to reset the column width or row height to the original setting, choose the **Format**, **Column**, **Standard Width** command.

Occasionally, you may find that the information in adjacent cells should actually be in the same cell. Instead of deleting the information from one cell and reentering it in the other cell, you can merge the cells.

A *font* is a particular typeface, and Excel allows you to establish the font's size. Various fonts and font sizes are accessible in the Formatting toolbar. You can use the fonts provided by Excel, as well as fonts designed especially for your printer. If Excel does not have a screen version of the printer font you select, it substitutes a font. When Excel makes a substitution, the printout looks different from the screen.

You can apply fonts to a single cell or a range of cells. You can also enhance fonts by using bold type, italics, and underlining and by changing font colors. Varying the font appearance and colors to emphasize data makes your worksheet more attractive. The Font Color button on the Formatting toolbar lets you change font colors in a snap. Of course, you must have a color monitor and a color printer to benefit from changing font colors.

In Excel, you can apply preset formats to selected data on a worksheet with the AutoFormat command. Generally, you apply one format at a time to a selected range. However, now you can apply a collection of formats supplied by Excel all at once. The formats help you create professional-looking financial reports, lists, and large tables.

One of the best ways to enhance the appearance of a worksheet is to add borders to the data on the worksheet. You can use the Borders button on the Formatting toolbar to add boxes around cells and ranges, and you can add emphasis lines anywhere on the worksheet.

Another way to change the overall worksheet display is to remove the gridlines that separate the cells in the worksheet. Your worksheet looks cleaner when you turn off the gridlines.

Automatically Formatting a Range

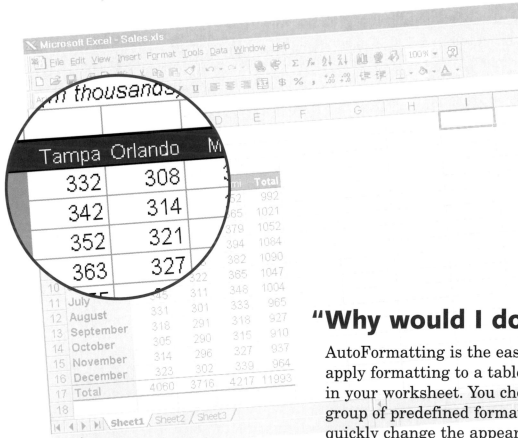

"Why would I do this?"

AutoFormatting is the easiest way to apply formatting to a table-like range in your worksheet. You choose from a group of predefined formats, which quickly change the appearance of data in a table, and Excel applies them to the specified range. These formats include many of the options you'll learn about individually in this section. You'll use options discussed in later tasks to format individual cells or small groups of cells.

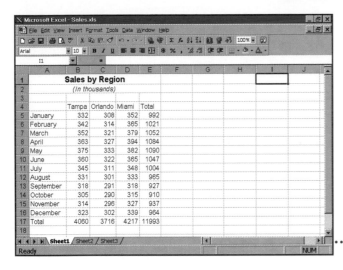

1 Open a new worksheet by clicking the **New** button on the Standard toolbar. Then enter the data you see in the figure shown here.

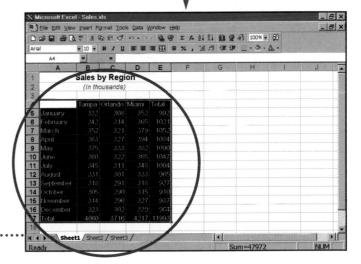

2 Select the range you want Excel to automatically format. For example, select the range **A4:E17**.

3 Select the **Format** menu and click **AutoFormat** to open the AutoFormat dialog box.

141

4 To preview a possible format for your table, click a choice in the **Table Format** list. For example, click **Colorful 1**. The Sample box changes to show the formatting for that option. You can preview as many formats as you want without applying any of them.

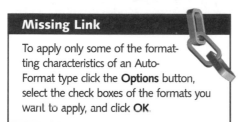

Missing Link

To apply only some of the formatting characteristics of an Auto-Format type click the **Options** button, select the check boxes of the formats you want to apply, and click **OK**.

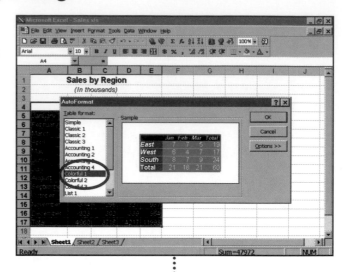

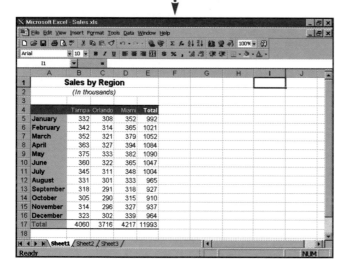

5 To apply formatting, click the option you want to apply and click **OK**. (For this example, select the **Classic 2** format.) ■

Puzzled?

If you don't like the results of AutoFormatting, click the **Undo** tool on the Standard toolbar, or reopen the AutoFormat dialog box and choose **None** from the **Table Format** list.

Formatting a Range Based on Conditions

"Why would I do this?"

Sometimes, you want to call attention to numbers that meet certain criteria. For example, take a look at the table you just autoformatted in Task 39. Suppose you want to highlight all the sales figures that exceed $350,000—you want them all to appear in red, for example. Or suppose you want sales figures between $350,000 and $375,000 to appear in red, and you want sales figures exceeding $375,000 to be blue.

You can use conditional formatting, which allows you to tell Excel to search for cells that match criteria you set and then format those cells as you indicate. You can set up to three conditions for Excel to use when searching, and you can apply font colors, borders, or cell patterns (such as background colors) to cells that meet your criteria.

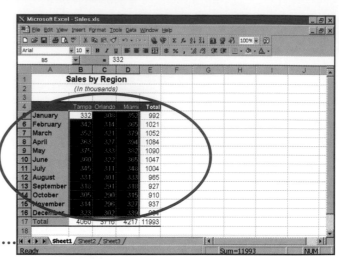

1 Select the cells you want Excel to compare to the criteria you will set. For this example, select **B5:D16**.

2 Select the **Format** menu and click **Conditional Formatting** to open the Conditional Formatting dialog box.

3 In the leftmost list box under **Condition 1**, choose what you want Excel to compare: a cell value or a formula. Choose **Cell Value Is**.

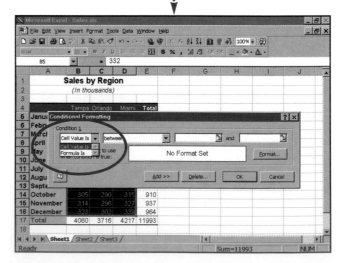

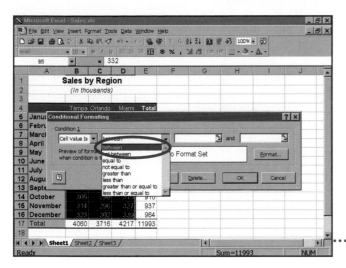

4 In the next list box, select **between** to tell Excel how you want cell values to compare to the criteria you're going to enter.

5 In the next two boxes, provide values for Excel to use for comparison. Type **350** and **375** in the two boxes. Click the **Format** button to display the Format Cells dialog box, in which you tell Excel what to do with cell values that meet your criteria.

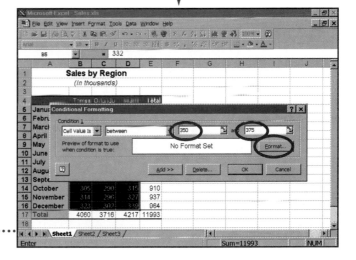

6 From each of the three tabs in the Format Cells dialog box, select the formatting you want to apply. For example, on the **Font** tab, open the **Color** drop-down list, and choose **Red** from the Color palette that appears. Then choose **Bold** from the **Font Style** list.

7 Click **OK** to return to the Conditional Formatting dialog box. The Preview box shows the effect of your formatting selections. To add another condition, click the **Add** button.

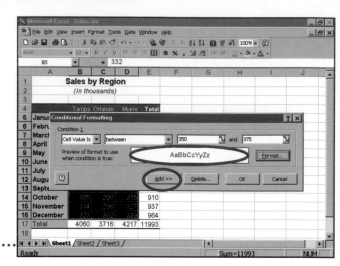

8 Excel displays a new area for Condition 2. Repeat steps 3–8 to set up **Cell Value Is Greater Than 375** for the second condition. Then use the Format Cells dialog box to set the formatting so that cells containing values greater than 375 will appear as bold white numbers (Font tab) on a shaded blue background (Patterns tab).

Missing Link

To delete a condition, click the **Delete** button, choose the condition to delete, and click **OK**.

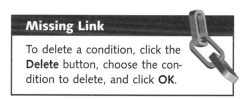

9 Click **OK** to apply your conditional formatting. Excel applies the formatting you specified to cells that meet your criteria. ■

Puzzled?

You can still modify conditions after you have set them and closed the dialog box. First click any cell that was part of the original selection, and then choose the **Format**, **Conditional Formatting** command. Excel reopens the dialog box, showing you the existing conditions for the cell.

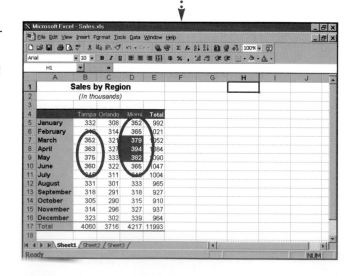

Aligning Text

"Why would I do this?"

When you enter data into a cell, numbers, dates, and times automatically align flush with the right side of the cell. Text entries, on the other hand, align flush with the left side of the cell. However, you can change the alignment of information at any time. For instance, you might want to fine-tune the appearance of column headings across columns. You can center a heading across more than one column, or you can right-align headings to line them up with the numbers that are right-aligned.

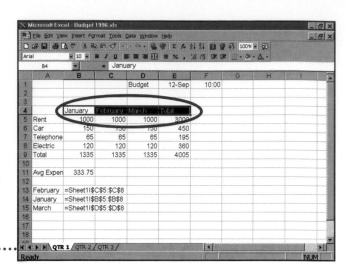

1 In the Budget worksheet, hold down the mouse button and drag the mouse to select cells **B4**, **C4**, **D4**, and **E4** (the range you want to right-align). Notice that the entries in these cells are left-aligned; that's the default when you enter labels.

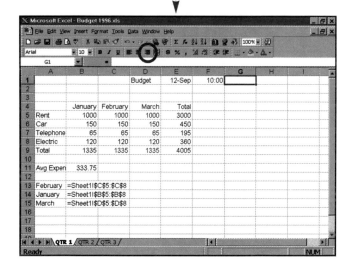

2 Click the **Align Right** button on the Formatting toolbar. Then click any cell to cancel the selection. Excel right-aligns the contents of each cell in the range. ■

Puzzled?
To undo your most recent alignment change, click the **Undo** button on the Standard toolbar.

Displaying Dollar Signs, Commas, and Percent Signs

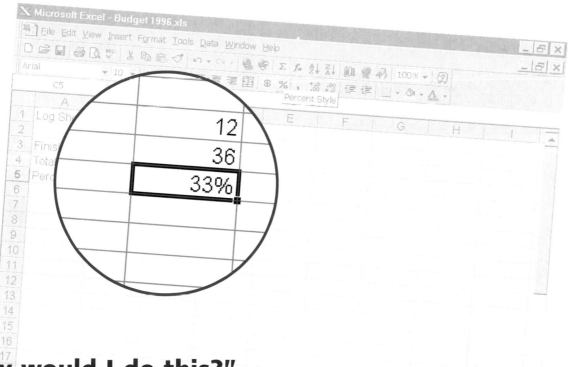

"Why would I do this?"

You can display numeric values in many ways in Excel. *Formatting* a number means to change the way Excel displays it. Excel offers many formatting options. For instance, you can format the number 600 to look like currency ($600.00) or to be a percent (600%). Remember, though, that it's important for the numbers in your worksheet to appear in the correct format. After all, $600.00 is certainly different from 600%!

Task 42: Displaying Dollar Signs, Commas, and Percent Signs

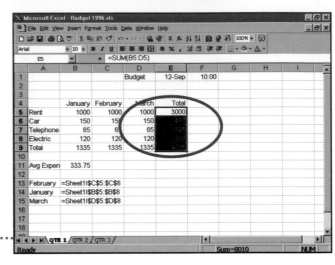

1 In the Budget worksheet, drag over the cells **E5** through **E9** to select the range in which you want to display dollar signs.

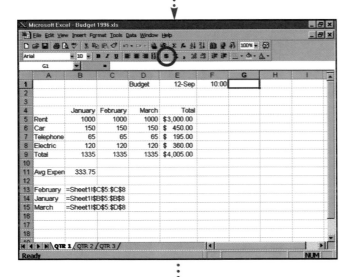

2 Click the **Currency Style** button on the Formatting toolbar, and then click any cell to cancel the selection. Excel formats the values with dollar signs, commas, and two decimal places.

Puzzled?

You might find that a column gets larger when you apply formatting. If necessary, Excel automatically adjusts column widths for you to account for the additional characters that formatting produces.

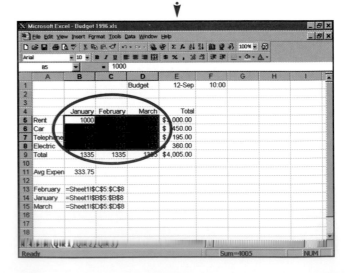

3 Drag over cells **B5** through **D8** to select the range in which you want to display commas but not dollar signs.

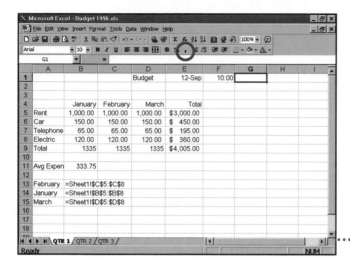

4 Click the **Comma Style** button on the Formatting toolbar. Then click any cell to clear the selection. When you do, Excel applies the changes, displaying the values with commas and two decimal places.

5 Click the **QTR 2** tab and, if you don't see the information shown in this figure, enter the information. (The formula in cell C5 is =C3/C4.) Click cell **C5**, the cell containing the value you want to display as a percentage.

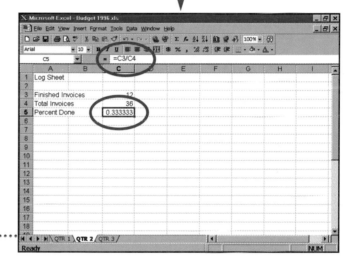

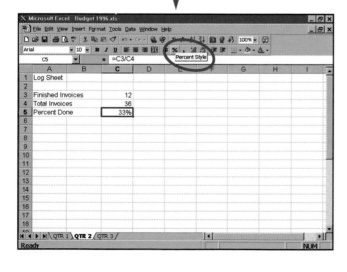

6 Click the **Percent Style** button on the Formatting toolbar. Excel displays the values with percent signs and zero decimal places. ■

Puzzled?

To undo your most recent formatting change, click the **Undo** button on the Standard toolbar.

151

Specifying Decimal Places

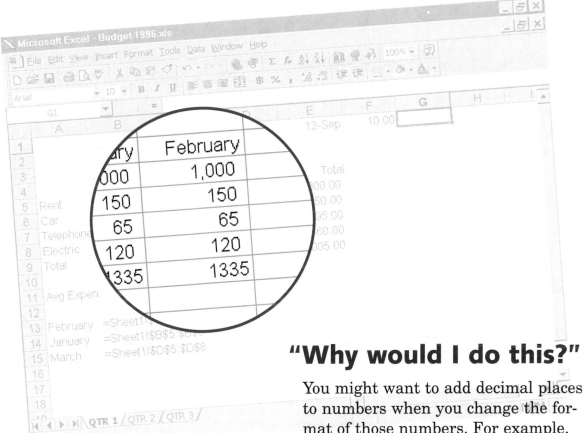

"Why would I do this?"

You might want to add decimal places to numbers when you change the format of those numbers. For example, Excel assumes you want two decimal places when you change the format to Currency. However, sometimes you don't want any decimal places, or you want a number of decimal places other than what's displayed. For example, if your Currency numbers aren't going to have cents, you don't need to display two decimal places. You can control how many decimal places appear in any given cell.

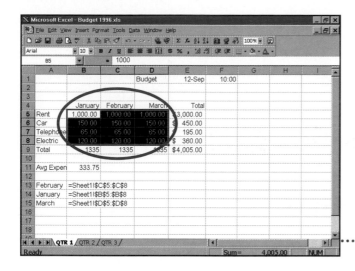

1 Click the **QTR 1** tab of the Budget worksheet. Then drag over cells **B5** through **D8** to select those cells as the range for which you want to specify decimal places.

2 Click the **Decrease Decimal** button on the Formatting toolbar twice. Each time you click the button, Excel moves the decimal point one place to the right. Click any cell to clear the selection. ■

Missing Link

If you select zero decimal places, Excel rounds the values to fit this format. For example, if you enter 7.5 in a cell, Excel rounds the number to 8 when formatting to zero decimal places.

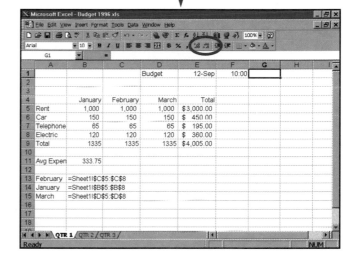

TASK

44

Changing Date and Time Formats

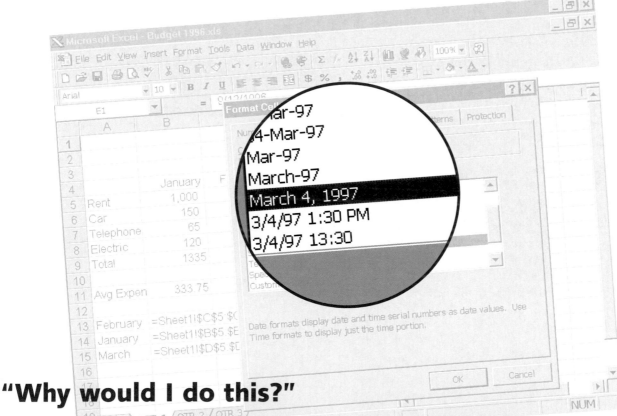

"Why would I do this?"

In Excel, you can enter dates in several different ways so that Excel accepts the date and displays it in a particular format. Likewise, you can change the way Excel displays the date and the time. For instance, if you prefer 9/12/1996 or September 12, 1996 over 12-Sep-1996,

change the date format. For times, Excel uses the 24-hour time format unless you enter an a.m. or p.m. designation. The time 10:00 in cell E1 of your budget might be clearer as 10:00 AM.

154

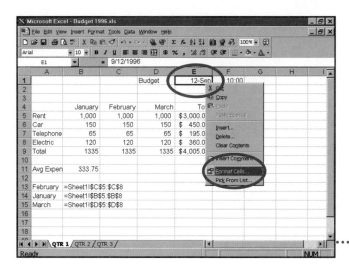

1 On the **QTR 1** tab, select cell **E1**. Then right-click the cell and choose **Format Cells** from the shortcut menu. Excel displays the Number tab in the Format Cells dialog box.

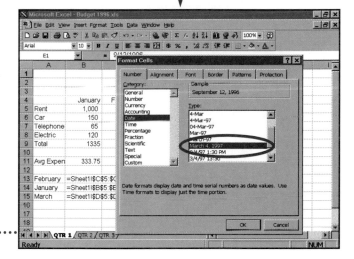

2 Because the selected cell is already formatted as a date, Excel selects Date in the Category list, and date formats appear in the Type list. Click **March 4, 1997** in the **Type** list. A sample appears at the top of the dialog box and uses the value in the selected cell to preview the format.

3 Click **OK** to accept the format choice. Excel displays the date in the new format and widens column E to accommodate the new format in cell E1.

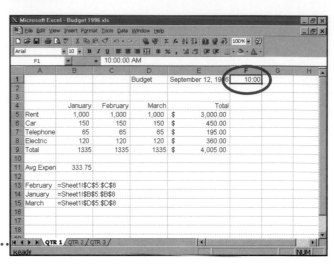

4 To change the appearance of the time shown in cell F1, select cell **F1** (the cell containing the time entry you want to format). Then press **Ctrl+1** (use the 1 above the typing keys, not on the numeric keypad), or select the **Format**, **Cells** command. Excel displays the Format Cells dialog box again.

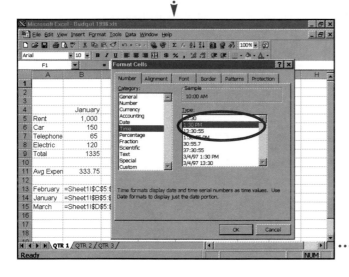

5 Because the cell is already formatted as a time, Excel selects Time in the Category list, and time formats appear in the Type list. In the **Type** list, click **1:30 PM** to tell Excel to display the time using a 12-hour clock and to include **AM** or **PM** when displaying the time. A sample appears at the top of the dialog box.

6 Click **OK** to accept the format choice. Excel displays the time in the new format: 10:00 AM. ■

Puzzled?

To undo your most recent formatting change, click the **Undo** button on the Standard toolbar.

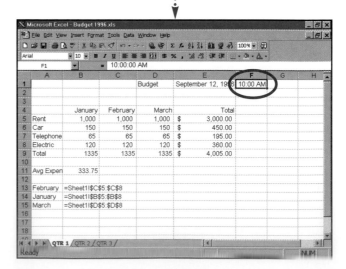

Copying Formats

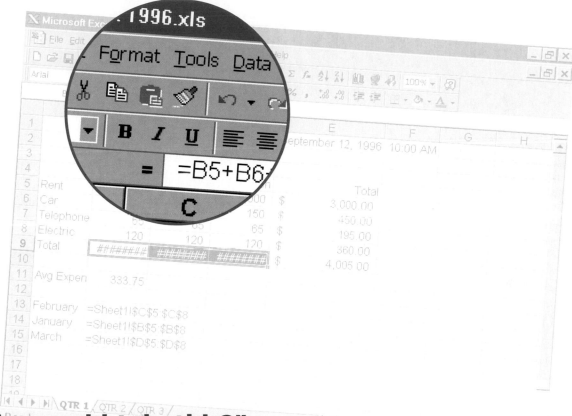

"Why would I do this?"

When you get a label or number formatted just the way you want it, you don't have to repeat the formatting process for every label or number you want to change to that format. You can save a lot of time by copying the formatting of one label or number to all the others that must match it. You can do this easily using the Format Painter button.

Task 45: Copying Formats

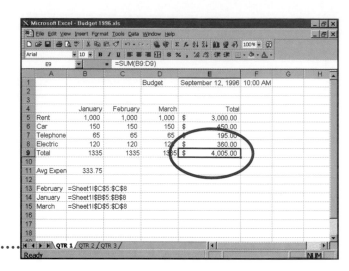

1 Select the cell that has the formatting you want to copy. For example, click cell **E9**, which has the Currency format.

2 Click the **Format Painter** button on the Standard toolbar. This button performs the functions of the Copy and Paste Format commands. A dashed copy marquee appears around cell E9.

Missing Link

To copy one set of formats to several locations, double-click the **Format Painter** button, and then select each cell that you want to format. When you finish copying formats, single-click the **Format Painter** button.

3 Drag over cells **B9, C9,** and **D9**. When you release the mouse button, Excel copies the format of cell E9 to B9 through D9. Click any cell to deselect the range. ■

Missing Link

If you see number signs (#) in the column, the entry is too long to fit in the column. You must change the column width, which you'll learn how to do in the next task.

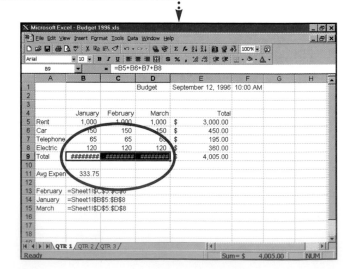

Changing Column Width and Row Height

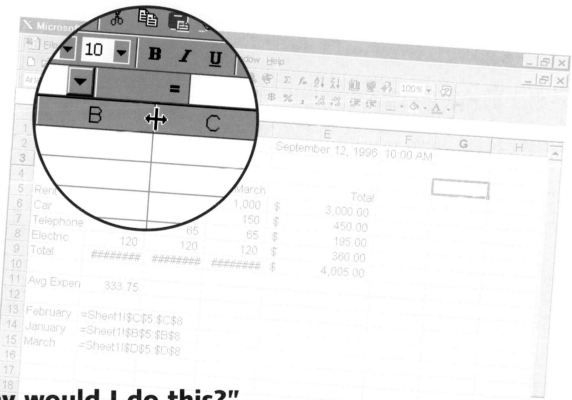

"Why would I do this?"

Number signs (#) in a cell indicate that the column is not wide enough to display either the results of a formula in the cell or additional formatting you've added to a number in the cell. Similarly, cut off letters or numbers indicate that a row is not tall enough to fully display the contents of its cells.

Often, the formatting (and the selected font) makes an entry larger than the default column width or row height. For example, the value $3,000 is only six characters. But if you format the number as currency with two decimal places, Excel displays it as $3,000.00, which then contains nine characters.

Task 46: Changing Column Width and Row Height

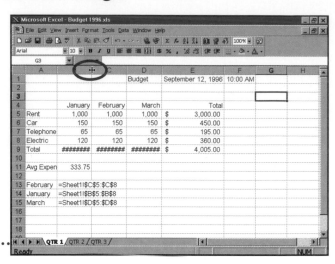

1 Position the mouse pointer in the column header area (where the column letters appear) on the line to the right of the column you want to widen. For example, place the mouse pointer on the line that separates column **B** from column **C** so you can widen column B. The mouse pointer changes to a two-headed arrow attached to a vertical black bar.

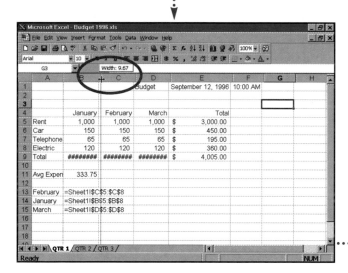

2 Hold down the mouse button and drag the mouse a small amount to the right. Excel widens the column. As you drag, you'll see a ScreenTip that indicates the column width in characters.

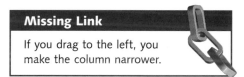

Missing Link

If you drag to the left, you make the column narrower.

3 To use the AutoFit feature place the mouse pointer in the column header area on the line to the right of column **C**. Double-click the line, and Excel adjusts the column width to accommodate the largest entry. Repeat this step for Column **D**. ■

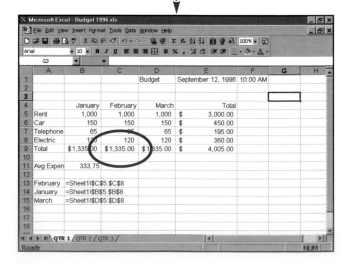

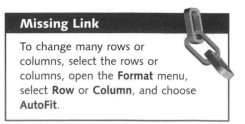

Missing Link

To change many rows or columns, select the rows or columns, open the **Format** menu, select **Row** or **Column**, and choose **AutoFit**.

Merging Cells in Columns or Rows

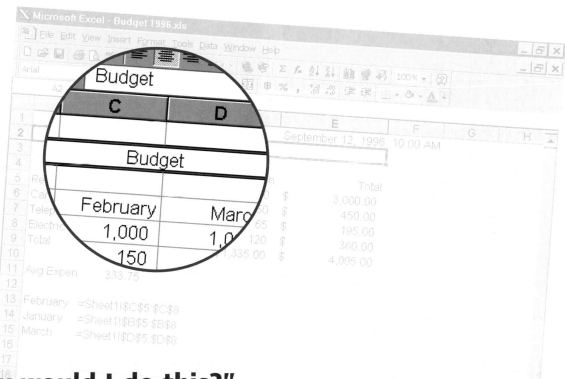

"Why would I do this?"

Suppose you decide you want to center a title for your workbook over a series of columns. For example, the Budget worksheet would look nice if you centered the word "Budget" over columns A through E. To do that, you merge cells so that you can center the word "budget" into one wide cell.

When you merge cells, you must first select the range of cells you want to

merge. It's important to remember that Excel will delete all data in the selected range except that which appears in the upper-left cell of the selection. So, for example, if you select A1:E1 to center "Budget" in row 1 over columns A through E, Excel would wipe out the date that appears in cell E1.

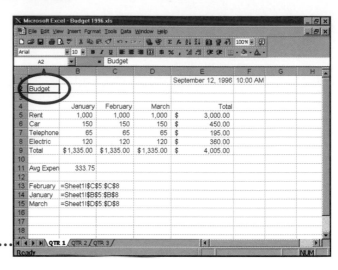

1 Move **Budget** to cell **A2**. You can cut and paste, or you can drag and drop.

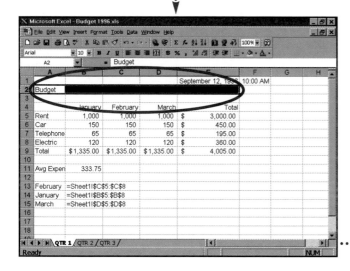

2 Select the range of cells you want to merge. In this example, you want to merge **A2:E2**.

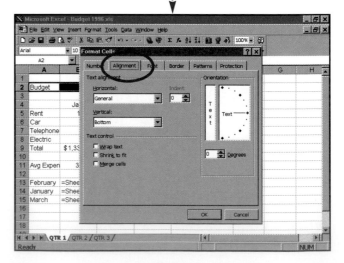

3 Select the **Format**, **Cells** command to display the Format Cells dialog box. Then click the **Alignment** tab.

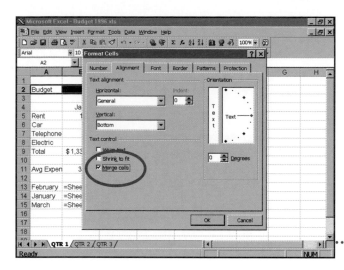

4 Click **Merge Cells** to place a check in the check box.

5 Click **OK** to close the Format Cells dialog box. Cell A2 now spans columns A through E.

Puzzled?

If you mistakenly merge the wrong group of cells, reopen the Format Cells dialog box, click the **Alignment** tab, and click to remove the check from the **Merge Cells** check box.

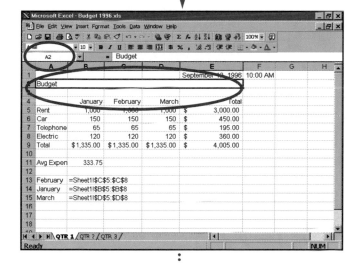

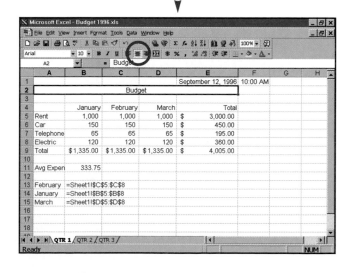

6 To center the cell's contents within the cell, click the **Center** alignment button. ■

Missing Link

As a shortcut, you can merge and center simultaneously. Select the range of cells you want to merge, and then click the **Merge and Center** button on the Formatting toolbar. (The Merge and Center button is two buttons to the right of the Center alignment button.)

Changing and Enhancing Fonts

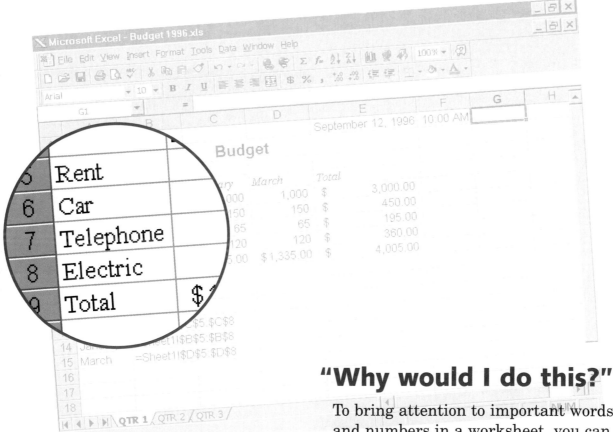

"Why would I do this?"

To bring attention to important words and numbers in a worksheet, you can change the font, font size, font style, and font color. For example, you can change the font for text in the body of your worksheet to Times New Roman in order to make reading easier. In addition, you can specify styles such as bold, italic, and underline to emphasize significant words and numbers.

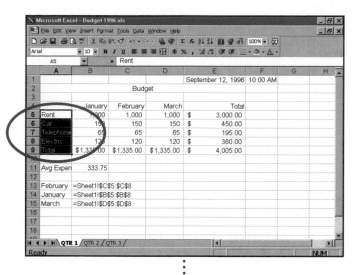

1 Select the text you want to change: cells **A5:A9**.

Missing Link

Desktop publishing guidelines suggest that you use *sans serif* fonts (such as Arial) for headlines and titles and that you use *serif* fonts (such as Times New Roman) for text in paragraphs and in the body of the worksheet. Sans serif fonts do not contain tails on the letters; serif fonts do contain tails. This type is a sans serif font.

2 Click the down arrow next to the **Font** box on the Formatting toolbar to display the list of available fonts.

Missing Link

The fonts in the list can vary from one computer to the next, depending on the type of printer and the fonts that are installed.

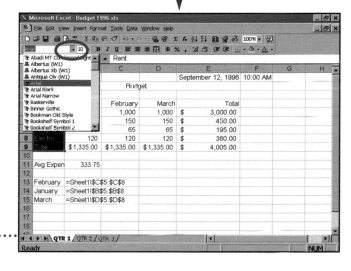

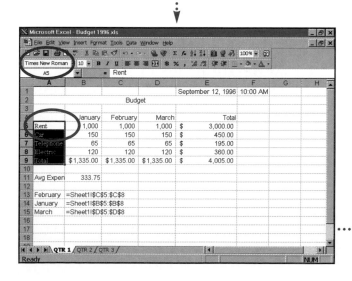

3 Click any font in the list to apply it to the selected text. In this case, choose **Times New Roman**. The text appears in the new font. Click any cell to cancel the selection.

Puzzled?

You can move quickly through the list of fonts by typing the first letter of the name of the font you want to choose. Excel scrolls through the list to display the first font that begins with that letter.

4 You might want to change the font size of the workbook title, making it larger to emphasize it. Select cell **A2,** and then click the down arrow next to the **Font Size** box on the Formatting toolbar. You'll see a list of font sizes.

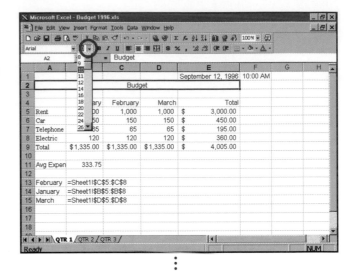

Missing Link

The font sizes in the list can vary from one computer to the next, depending on the type of printer and the fonts that are installed.

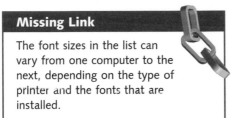

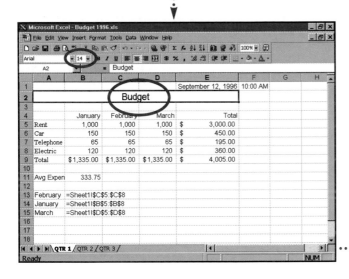

5 Click a larger font size, such as **14**, to change the font size for the title.

Missing Link

You also can click in the **Font** text box and type any font size from 1 to 409.

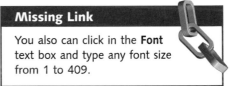

6 To draw even more attention to the title, click the **Bold** button on the Formatting toolbar. Excel applies bold to the selected cells—in this case, A2.

Missing Link

To apply the formatting you just selected to other text in the worksheet, use the Format Painter tool on the Formatting toolbar (as described in Task 45).

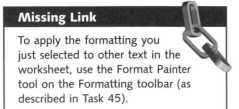

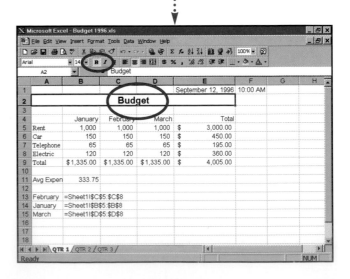

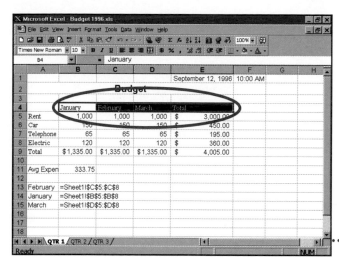

7 Next, add italics to the titles in row 4. First, select cells **B4:E4**.

8 Click the **Italic** button on the Formatting toolbar to apply italics to the selected cells. Then click any cell to clear the selection so you can see the changes more clearly. ■

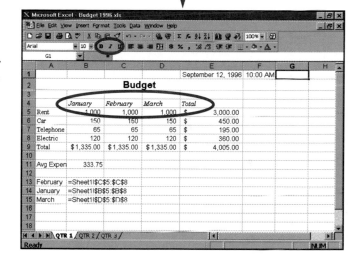

Missing Link

To remove the bold or italic style, select the cells that contain the style and click either the **Bold** button or the **Italic** button on the Formatting toolbar.

Using Cell Comments

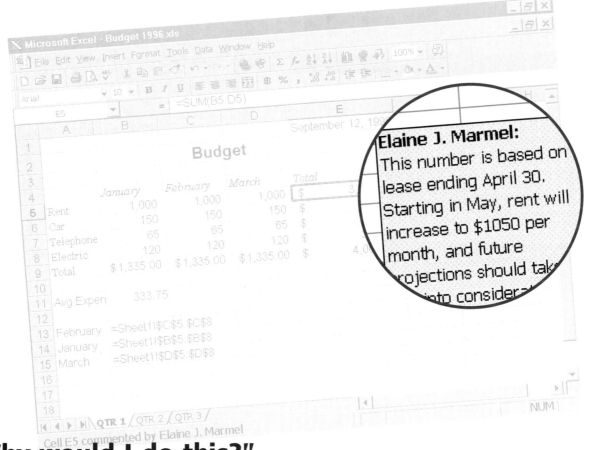

"Why would I do this?"

Suppose you decide you want to annotate the information in your worksheet. Maybe you want to explain "how" you got a particular number. In Excel 97, you can attach notes—called *cell comments*—to cells in your worksheet. Then anyone who looks at or uses your worksheet within Excel can point to a comment and read it. In addition, you can choose to have Excel print these notes when you print the worksheet so that anyone who looks at the hard copy can also see your comments.

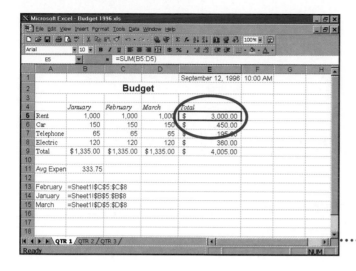

1 Click cell **E5** to place an explanatory note about rent there.

2 Open the **Insert** menu and choose the **Comment** command. Excel displays a graphic text box, and the insertion point appears in the text box.

Puzzled?

When you type, you do not need to press Enter at the end of a line. Excel scrolls down to allow you to type more text in the box.

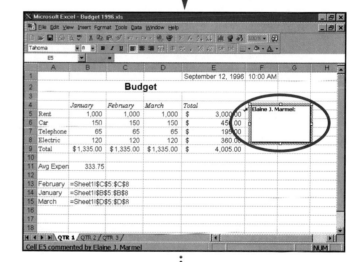

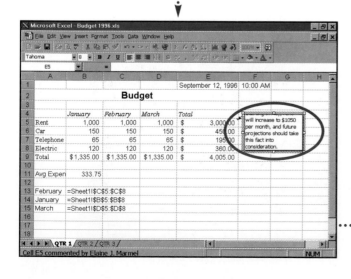

3 Type whatever text you want to attach to the current cell. For example, type **This number is based on a lease ending April 30. Starting in May, rent will increase to $1050 per month, and future projections should take this fact into consideration.**

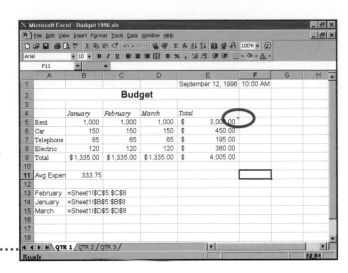

4 Click any where in the worksheet to close the graphic text box. Excel displays a small red marker in the upper-right corner of the cell containing the comment.

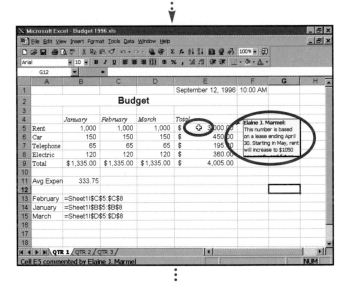

5 To see the cell comment, position the mouse pointer over any cell that has a red marker in the upper-right corner. In this case, point to cell **E5**, and Excel displays the cell comment.

Missing Link

Although you were able to type beyond the boundary of the text box, Excel displays only the portion of the comment visible within the standard-size box. To enlarge the box so you can see all of the comment, refer to step 7.

6 To have Excel display a particular comment all of the time, right-click the cell it's in and choose **Show Comment** from the shortcut menu. To hide a particular comment, right-click the cell and choose **Hide Comment**.

Missing Link

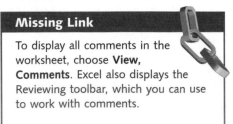

To display all comments in the worksheet, choose **View, Comments**. Excel also displays the Reviewing toolbar, which you can use to work with comments.

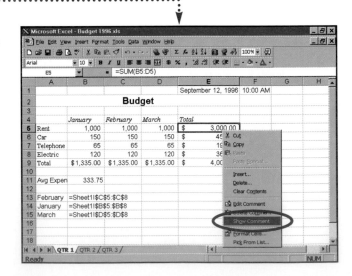

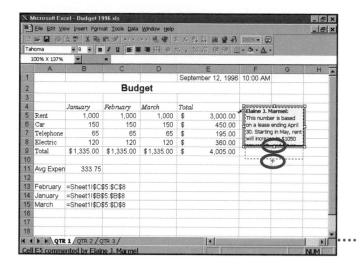

7 To edit a comment, display the comment and then right-click it. Excel redisplays the original text box. Edit the text or size the box as necessary. To enlarge the text box so the entire comment is visible, position the mouse pointer over the bottom handle of the text box. When the mouse pointer changes to a two-headed arrow, drag the handle downward.

8 To print cell comments, click in the worksheet containing the comment—in this case **QTR 1**. Then select the **File**, **Page Setup** command. In the Page Setup dialog box, click the **Sheet** tab.

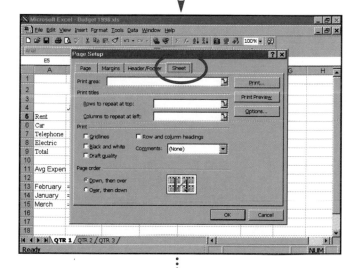

Puzzled?

To remove a note from a worksheet, right-click the cell containing the note you want to delete and choose **Delete Comment** from the shortcut menu.

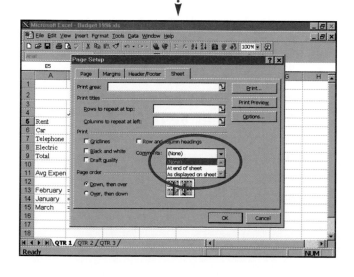

9 Open the **Comments** list box and indicate whether you want to print comments where they appear in your worksheet or at the end of the worksheet. If you want to print comments where they appear on the sheet, you must display the comments, and the entire comment must be visible. You can, however, print comments at the end of the sheet without displaying the comments. ■

Shading Cells

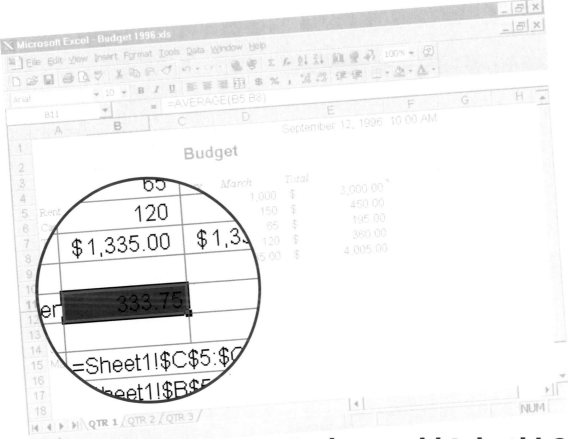

"Why would I do this?"

You can shade cells to draw attention to certain text or numbers in your worksheet. You might want to shade a high or low sales figure, an average, or a grand total, for instance. Shading can also help you distinguish numbers on a spreadsheet.

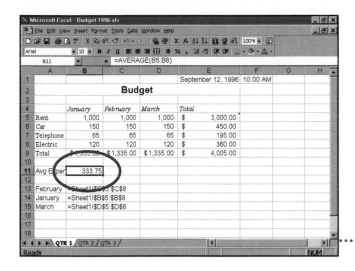

1 Click cell **B11** to indicate that it is the cell you want to shade.

2 Click the **Fill Color** drop-down arrow on the Formatting toolbar to display a color palette.

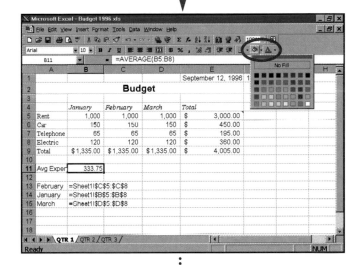

> ### Missing Link
>
> Depending on your printer, the shading might print differently than it appears on-screen—or it might not at all. If you don't have a color printer, shading with colors could actually block out the information in your worksheet. For printing on black-and-white printers, use shades of gray when shading.

3 In the first column of the color palette, click the third color from the top: red. Excel displays the shading in cell B11. ■

> ### Puzzled?
>
> To remove shading you just applied, immediately click the **Undo** button on the Standard toolbar, or click the **Fill Color** drop-down arrow and choose **No Fill**.

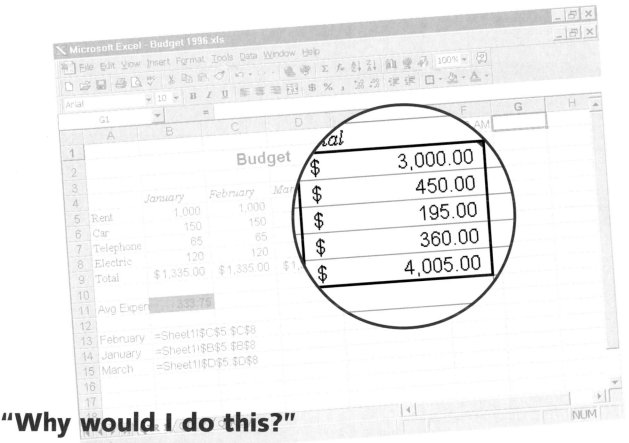

Adding Borders

"Why would I do this?"

Excel's Border command lets you add boxes around cells and ranges with either a single or double line. For example, you can add a single outline border to a cell to create a box that sets apart the title of the worksheet. Or you can add a double underline to the bottom of certain cells to bring attention to the totals they contain.

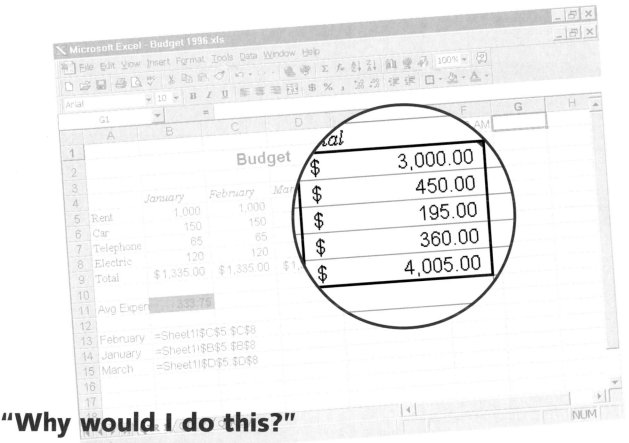

174

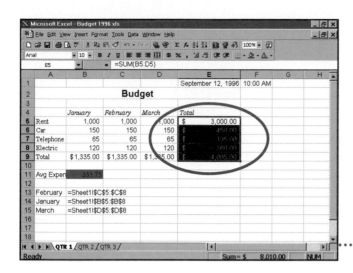

1 Select cells **E5** to **E9** to indicate the range you want to outline.

2 Click the **Borders** drop-down arrow on the Formatting toolbar to display a palette of border samples.

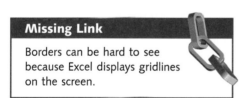

Missing Link

Borders can be hard to see because Excel displays gridlines on the screen.

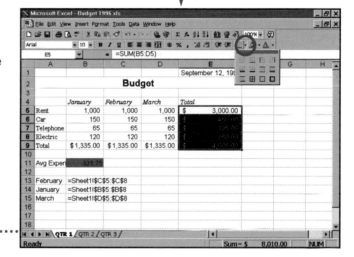

3 To have Excel outline the edges of the range with a thick single line, click the last border sample in the last row of the palette. Then click any other cell to deselect the range so you can see the outline. ■

Puzzled?

To remove the outline, immediately click the **Undo** button on the Standard toolbar, or click the **Borders** drop-down arrow and choose the first option.

Turning Off Gridlines

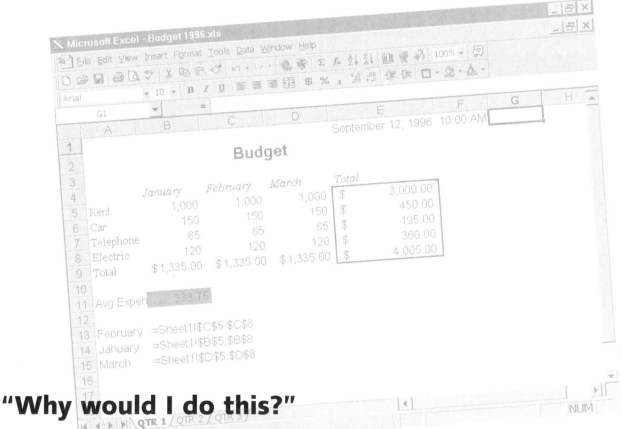

"Why would I do this?"

Another way to make your worksheet look more attractive is to turn off the gridlines that separate the cells in the worksheet. Sometimes your worksheet seems cleaner when displayed on the white background without the grids. Or you might want to turn off gridlines in your worksheets so you can see how the data will look when printed on white paper.

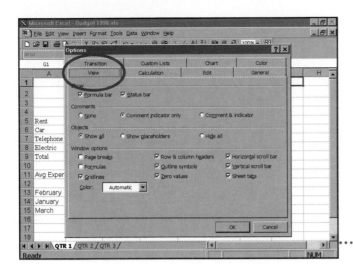

1 Open the **Tools** menu and select **Options**. Click the **View** tab, and Excel displays the View options in the Options dialog box.

2 In the Window Options area, click the **Gridlines** check box to remove the check mark (which turns off the gridlines).

Missing Link

When you turn off gridlines, you turn them off for only the active worksheet. To turn off gridlines for other sheets in the workbook, you have to select each sheet and repeat these steps.

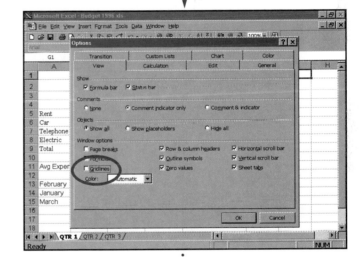

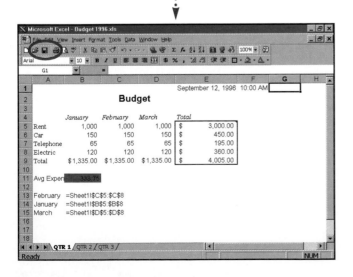

3 Click **OK**, and the gridlines no longer appear in the worksheet. Click the **Save** button on the Standard toolbar to save the file without the gridlines. ■

Puzzled?

If you change your mind and want to turn on the gridlines again, repeat these steps but place a check mark in **Gridlines** check box.

PART VI

Printing the Worksheet

I N EXCEL, YOU CAN PRINT YOUR WORKSHEETS using a basic printing procedure, or you can enhance the printout using several print options. It is fairly simple to print a worksheet in Excel.

First you set up the format for your printout. You can insert manual page breaks in your worksheet to split the worksheet into two or more pages. If you don't, Excel automatically sets the page breaks. Manual page breaks override Excel's automatic page breaks, and they remain in the worksheet until you remove them.

You will find most print options in the Page Setup dialog box, which contains four tabs of options: Page, Margins, Header/Footer, and Sheet. Excel offers several important Sheet options that you might find useful. You can tell Excel what part of the worksheet you want to print using the Print Area option. For large worksheets, you might want to print headings for each column at the top of each page, which you do with the Rows to Repeat at Top option. Likewise, you can print headings for each row at the left side of each page by using the Columns to Repeat at Left option.

With Excel's Print Preview feature, you can review the appearance of the worksheet before you commit it to paper. The first page of the worksheet appears as a reduced image in the Print Preview screen. However, you can use the Zoom feature in Print Preview to magnify the view so you can inspect the printout more closely. When you click the Zoom button again, Excel reduces the view back to a smaller image. From the Preview window, you can also change the margins and page setup, preview where page breaks will occur and adjust them if necessary, and start printing. See your Microsoft Excel documentation for complete information.

The Page and Margins options in the Page Setup dialog box control print enhancements such as orientation, margins, and the size of the paper you use. The default print orientation is Portrait, which means that the worksheet will be printed vertically on the paper. You can choose Landscape to print the worksheet sideways (horizontally) on the paper.

If the worksheet is too wide, you can try decreasing the widths of some cells if possible. If the worksheet is still too large to print on one page, you can change the top, bottom, left, and right margins, or you can try reducing the printout using the Adjust To option in the Page Setup dialog box.

The Fit To option prints the worksheet at a size that fits the size of the page. You can enter the number of pages in the Page(s) Wide By text box and the Tall text box to specify the document's width and height. This is especially useful for printing graphics and charts; however, this option may not be available on all printers. You may need to experiment with all the print options until you get the results you want.

Excel lets you add headers and footers to print information at the top and bottom of every page of the printout. You can choose the headers and footers suggested by Excel, or you can include any text plus special commands to control the appearance of the header or footer.

It is a good idea to save your worksheets before printing—just in case a printer error or other problem occurs. This ensures that you won't lose any changes you've made since the last time you saved the worksheet.

This part introduces you to the basics of printing the worksheet. With some experimentation and practice, you will be able to create some very interesting printed results.

TASK 53

Inserting and Removing Page Breaks

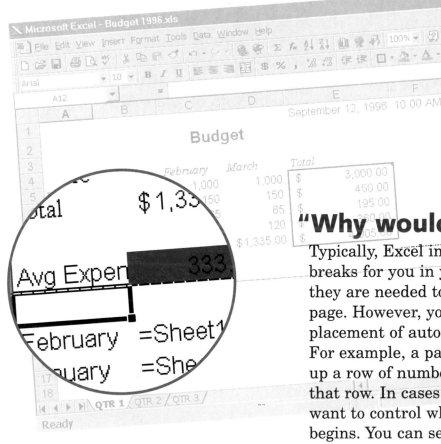

"Why would I do this?"

Typically, Excel inserts automatic page breaks for you in your worksheet as they are needed to fit on the printed page. However, you may not like the placement of automatic page breaks. For example, a page break might split up a row of numbers and the sum of that row. In cases like this one, you'll want to control where each new page begins. You can set a manual page break anywhere on the worksheet. A manual page break overrides the automatic page break entered by Excel.

You won't be able to perform this task unless a printer is installed. If no printer is installed, refer to your Windows manual.

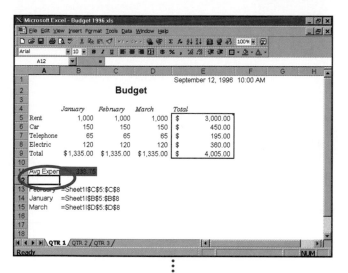

1 Click the first cell you want to appear on a new page (after the page break). For example, click cell **A12**. Excel will print everything above row 12 on one page, and will print row 12 and everything below it on the next page.

Missing Link

Whether you are inserting a vertical or horizontal page break, you make the active cell the first cell you want to appear on a new page.

2 Open the **Insert** menu and select **Page Break**. Excel enters the manual page break above the active cell.

Missing Link

To insert a manual page break both above and to the left of the selected cell, click a cell that is not in the far left column of the worksheet.

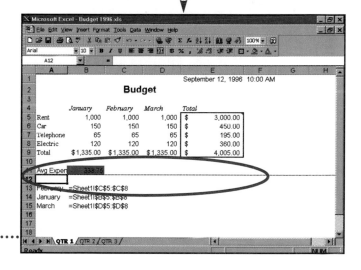

3 To remove a manual page break, make sure the active cell is immediately below and to the right of the page break line(s). Then select the **Insert**, **Remove Page Break** command. The manual page break disappears from above the active cell. ■

Missing Link

On-screen, manual page breaks are displayed as longer, thicker dashed lines than automatic page breaks.

183

Selecting a Print Area

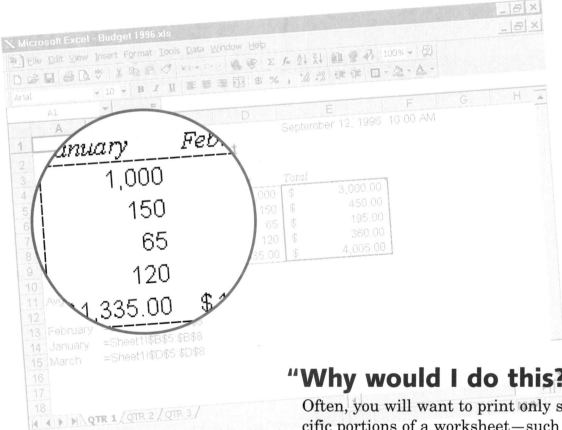

"Why would I do this?"

Often, you will want to print only specific portions of a worksheet—such as a range of cells. To do that, you can single out an area as a separate page and then print only that page. Excel will print only the established print area. However, if the area is too large to fit on one page, Excel will break it into multiple pages.

You won't be able to perform this task unless a printer is installed. If no printer is installed, refer to your Windows manual.

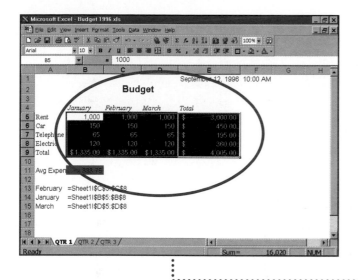

1 Select the range you want to set as the print area. For this example, select the range **B5:E9** as the print area.

Puzzled?

Do not include the title, subtitle, or column and row headings in the print area. If you do, Excel will print the labels twice. (In the next task, you will use the labels to print the column and row headings on every page.)

2 Open the **File** menu, select **Print Area**, and choose **Set Print Area** from the submenu. Then click any cell to clear the selection. As you can see, the print area (B5:E9) is now surrounded by a dotted line.

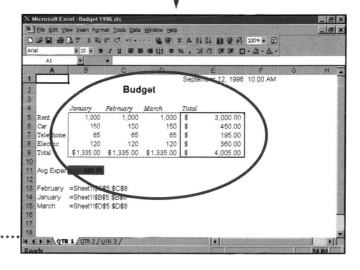

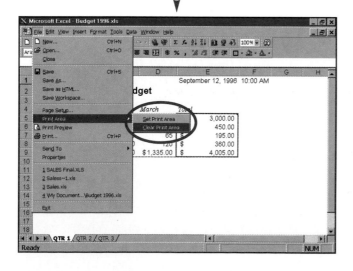

3 To remove the print area, open the **File** menu, select **Print Area**, and choose **Clear Print Area** from the submenu. ■

Missing Link

If everything looks okay, you can print your worksheet by clicking the **Print** button on the Standard toolbar.

185

55

Printing Column and Row Headings

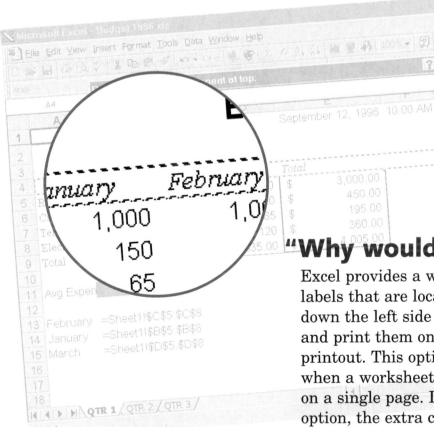

"Why would I do this?"

Excel provides a way for you to select labels that are located along the top and down the left side of your worksheet and print them on every page of the printout. This option is very useful when a worksheet is too wide to print on a single page. If you don't use this option, the extra columns and rows will be printed on subsequent pages without any labels—and you'll have a hard time matching numbers to row and column headings on the first page.

You won't be able to perform this task unless a printer is installed. If no printer is installed, refer to your Windows manual.

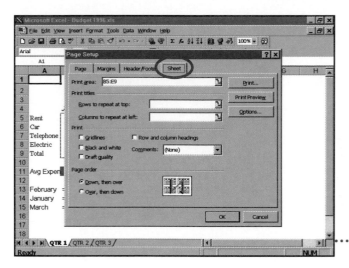

1 Open the **File** menu and select **Page Setup**. In the Page Setup dialog box, click the **Sheet** tab.

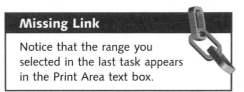

Missing Link

Notice that the range you selected in the last task appears in the Print Area text box.

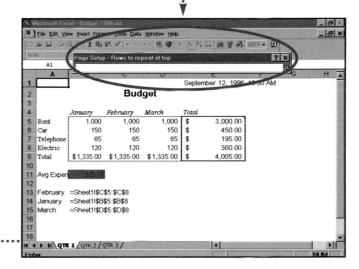

2 Click the **Collapse Dialog** button at the right end of the **Rows to Repeat at Top** text box. Excel collapses the Page Setup dialog box so you can see the worksheet.

3 To specify the headings you want to repeat at the top of every page, click anywhere in row **4**. Excel displays **$4:$4** in the collapsed Page Setup dialog box, and a dashed line appears around the row in the worksheet.

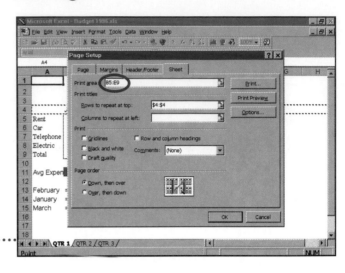

4 Click the **Collapse Dialog** button again to redisplay the Page Setup dialog box. The address of the selected range now appears in the Rows to Repeat at Top text box.

5 To specify the headings you want to repeat down the left side of every page, click the **Collapse Dialog** button in the **Columns to Repeat at Left** text box. Excel collapses the Page Setup dialog box so you can see the worksheet. Click anywhere in column **A**. Excel displays **$A:$E** in the text box, and a dashed line appears around the columns A–E.

> **Puzzled?**
>
> Although you clicked only column A, Excel selected A–E because cell A2 is a merged cell that spans columns A–E.

6 Click the **Collapse Dialog** button to redisplay the Page Setup dialog box with the selected range in the **Columns to Repeat at Left** text box and change the range address to **AA**. Click **OK** to close the dialog box, or click **Print** to print the worksheet with these settings. ■

> **Puzzled?**
>
> To remove the repeated rows and columns, delete the cell addresses in the **Rows to Repeat at Top** and **Columns to Repeat at Left** text boxes.

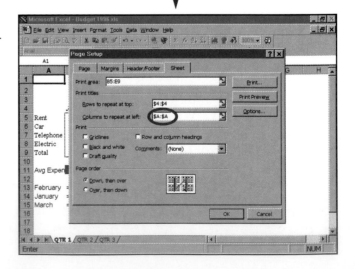

TASK 56

Adding Headers and Footers

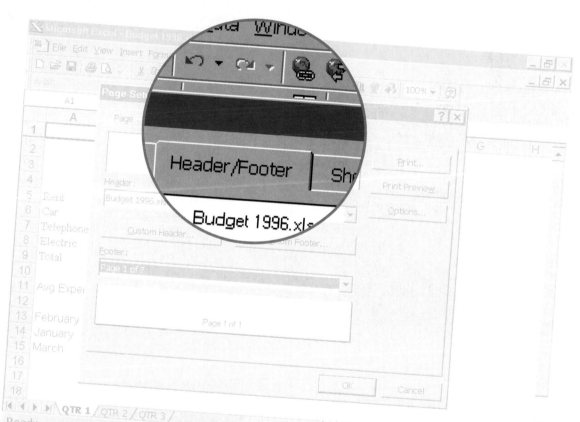

"Why would I do this?"

Headers and footers are lines of text that Excel prints on every page in a print job—headers at the top, footers at the bottom. You can include any text, the current date and time, or the file name, and you can even format the information. Headers and footers typically help the reader determine things

like "Which report am I reading?," "What page am I on?," or "When was this report created?"

You won't be able to perform this task unless a printer is installed. If no printer is installed, refer to your Windows manual.

1 Suppose you want to create a header that contains the name of your file, and you want to create a footer that will number the pages in your budget worksheet. Open the **File** menu, select **Page Setup**, and click the **Header/Footer** tab in the Page Setup dialog box to display the Header/Footer options.

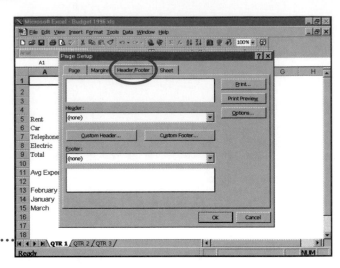

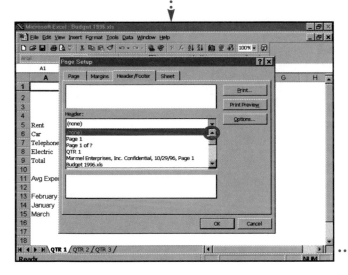

2 Click the **Header** drop-down arrow, and a list of suggested header information appears.

3 Scroll through the list if necessary, and click **Budget 1996.xls**. The sample header appears at the top of the box. Notice that "Budget 1996.xls" is centered.

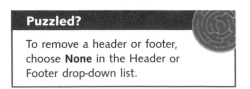

Puzzled?

To remove a header or footer, choose **None** in the Header or Footer drop-down list.

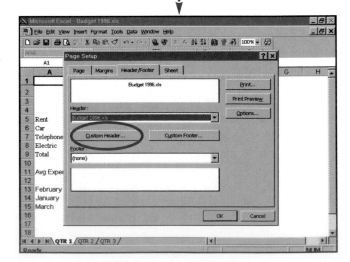

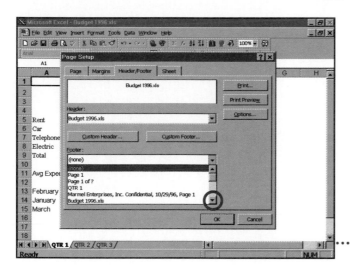

4 To add a footer, click the down arrow next to the **Footer** text box. A list of suggested footer information appears.

5 Scroll through the list (if necessary) and click **Page 1 of ?**. The sample footer appears centered at the bottom of the box. Click **OK** to close the Page Setup dialog box and enter your settings. ■

Puzzled?

Normally, you won't see the header and footer on-screen. To do so, you must preview the worksheet, which you will learn how to do in the next task.

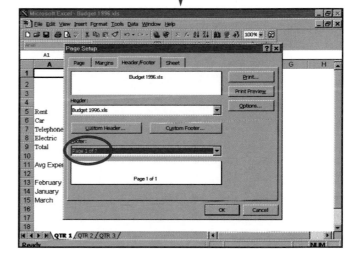

Previewing the Print Job

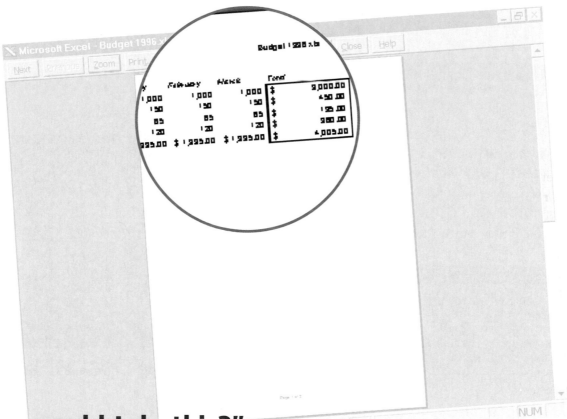

"Why would I do this?"

The Print Preview command lets you see worksheet pages on-screen as they will appear when printed on paper— including page numbers, headers, footers, fonts, fonts sizes and styles, orientation, and margins. It also enables you to preview the page breaks in a worksheet, so you can see where they will fall and adjust them if necessary.

Previewing your worksheet is a great way to catch formatting errors such as incorrect margins, overlapped data, bold data that's not supposed to be, and other problem text enhancements. You will save costly printer paper and time by first previewing your worksheet.

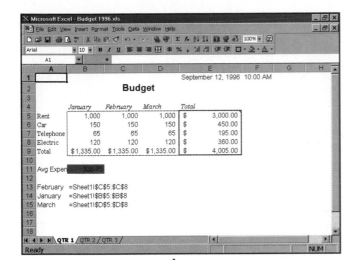

1 Click the **Print Preview** button on the Standard toolbar.

Missing Link

To preview the worksheet, you must have a printer installed and your monitor must have graphics capability. If you get an error message, either you don't have a printer installed or your monitor probably cannot display the worksheet. Install a printer and print the worksheet to see how it looks.

2 You will see a preview of how your worksheet will look when you print it. Click the **Zoom** button at the top of the screen.

Missing Link

You can also zoom by clicking anywhere on the Print Preview page. As you can see in this figure, the mouse pointer changes to look like a magnifying glass as you move it over the page.

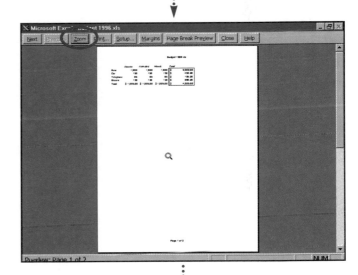

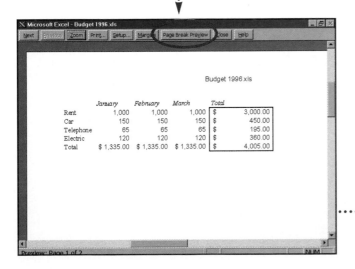

3 When you Zoom, you enlarge the preview to its actual size. By zooming the worksheet to actual size, you can examine the printout more closely. Click **Zoom** again to return to the original Print Preview size. Now check page breaks. Click **Page Break Preview** to see how Excel intends to break up your printout.

4 Initially, you'll see a dialog box explaining that you can adjust where page breaks occur by dragging. Click **OK**, and Excel displays your screen in a format similar to the one in this figure. You can see each page printed in gray. In the figure, Excel prints only one page—so you don't see any additional page breaks. Click the **Print Preview** button on the Standard toolbar to return to Print Preview.

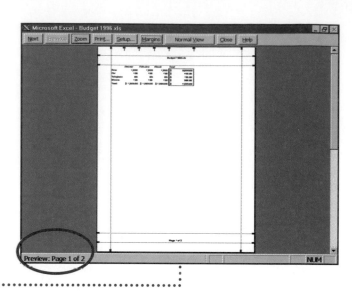

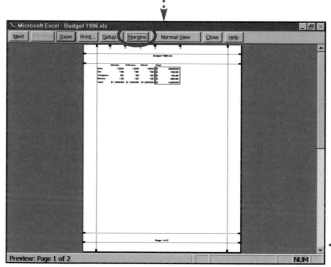

5 Click the **Margins** button to display markers that you can drag to adjust the margins. When you finish, click the **Margins** button again to hide the markers.

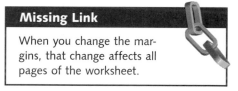

Missing Link

When you change the margins, that change affects all pages of the worksheet.

6 To exit the preview, click the **Normal View** button or the **Close** button. ■

Missing Link

You can also press the **Esc** key to quit the preview. If the Normal View button appears on the toolbar but you click the **Close** button instead, Excel redisplays the worksheet in Page Break Preview. To return to Normal view from there, use the **View**, **Normal** command.

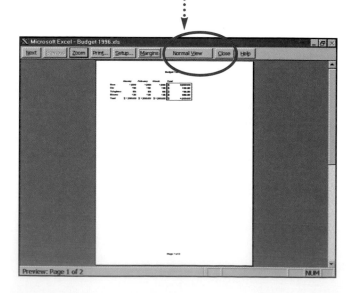

Printing the Worksheet

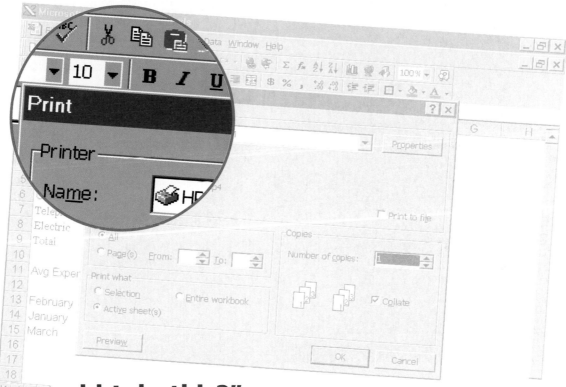

"Why would I do this?"

Excel gives you many print options for customizing the way you print your worksheets. You can change the orientation and the margins, or you can reduce or enlarge the printout to fit on an 8 1/2-by-11-inch sheet of paper. If you change some of these options, you may make the spreadsheet easier to read. The last thing you want to do is intimidate someone with a spreadsheet; they

might be likely to skip over things. Refer to your Microsoft Excel documentation for complete information on the options in the Page Setup dialog box.

You won't be able to perform this task unless a printer is installed. If no printer is installed, refer to your Windows manual.

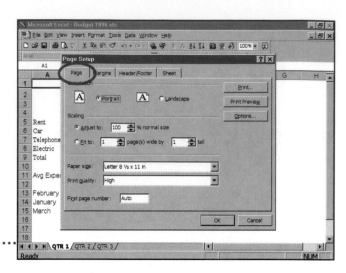

1 So you're ready to print the budget worksheet. Open the **File** menu and choose **Page Setup**. In the Page Setup dialog box, click the **Page** tab to display the Page options.

2 Click the **Landscape** option button to select Landscape orientation, which tells Excel to print the worksheet sideways.

Missing Link

If you don't need to set any special printing options, you can print the worksheet just by clicking the **Print** button in the Standard toolbar. (It's the fourth button from the left.)

3 Click the **Margins** tab to display the Margins options. By default, Excel uses the following margin settings: Left .75", Right .75", Top 1", Bottom 1", Header .5", and Footer .5". Double-click the **Top** text box and type **2** to reset the top margin at two inches.

Missing Link

You can click the spinner buttons at the edge of any box to increment or decrement that margin setting.

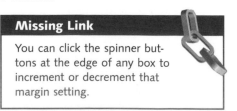

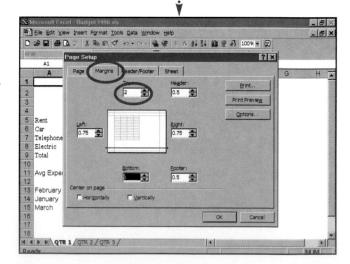

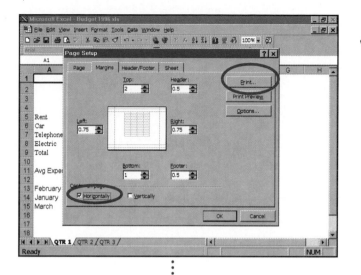

4 In the Center on Page area, click the **Horizontally** check box. Excel will center the page between the left and right margins, based on the current left and right margin settings.

Missing Link

You can see that the worksheet is centered horizontally in the preview sample in the middle of the dialog box.

5 To print the worksheet, click the **Print** button. Excel displays the Print dialog box, with the name of your printer at the top. Click **OK** to start the print job. ■

Puzzled?

To reset any options in the Page Setup dialog box, you have to repeat this procedure; you cannot use the Undo feature to reverse the settings. While Excel is actually printing, it displays a dialog box on-screen. To stop the print job at that point, click **Cancel**.

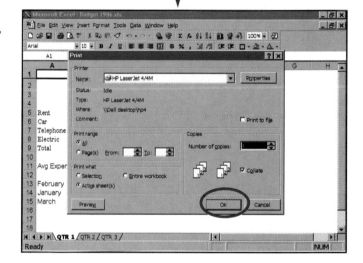

PART VII

Working with Charts

▲ ● ■ ■ ● ■ ▲ ●

BEFORE YOU CREATE A CHART, you should familiarize yourself with the elements of a chart. With the exception of pie charts, all charts contain at least two axes—one vertical axis and a horizontal axis (pie charts contain no axes, and some charts contain more than one vertical or horizontal axis). The *y-axis* is the vertical axis; Excel also refers to this axis as the *value axis* because it displays the values of the information you plot. The *x-axis* is the horizontal axis; Excel also refers to this axis as the *category axis,* because it contains divisions or classifications of information (categories) about your data. You'll learn more about categories in a moment.

Think of the values in worksheet cells as data points. Data points are grouped into bars, pie slices, lines, or other elements on a chart. We refer to each of these grouped data points as a *data series*. You'll see labels describing each data series in the legend of the chart. Suppose you were viewing a column chart containing three bars: one for January sales, one for February sales, and one for March sales. Although the chart has three bars, it contains only one data series: monthly sales.

Categories show the number of elements in a data series. You might use two data series to compare the sales of two different offices, and you might use four categories to compare these sales over four quarters. On such a chart, sales dollars would appear on the value axis (the vertical or y-axis); each office's name would appear in the legend of the chart (representing a data series); and Quarters 1–4 would appear as categories on the category axis (the horizontal or x-axis). Categories usually correspond to the number of columns that you have selected in your worksheet. *Category labels* describe the categories below the horizontal axis. These labels come from the column headings of the data you include in the chart.

The *chart text* includes all the labels on the chart. Most chart text has to be added to the basic chart. You can also format labels by changing the fonts, font sizes, font styles, and colors. Text is useful for explaining various elements on the chart.

The *plot area* consists of the actual bars, lines, or other elements that represent the data series. Everything outside the plot area helps explain what is inside the plot area. You can format the plot area by changing the patterns and colors of the data series. A *legend* contains the labels for the data series in the chart and serves as a "key" to the chart. To create the legend, Excel uses row labels it finds in the first column of the chart range. On the chart, the legend appears to the right of the chart data. However, you can move the legend anywhere you want on the chart—or even remove it completely. *Gridlines* are dotted lines you can add to a chart so that you can read the plotted data more easily. You can create three types of gridlines: horizontal, vertical, and a combination of both. After you add the gridlines, you can change their colors and patterns.

As you create a chart you'll see the Chart Options dialog box, which contains six tabs. Although you won't learn how to use all six tabs in this book, the table below gives you a brief idea of what you can do on each tab.

Tab	Description
Titles	Add or change the Chart title, Category (X) axis title, and Value (Y) axis title. If your chart type uses second category or value axes, you can add or change these titles, too.
Axes	Change the appearance of the category and value axes.
Gridlines	Determine whether both major and minor gridlines appear for the category and value axes.
Legend	Hide the legend or change its placement.
Data Labels	Add labels for each data point in a data series, and determine the type of label.
Data Table	Display or hide the underlying data that comprises the chart.

Creating a Chart

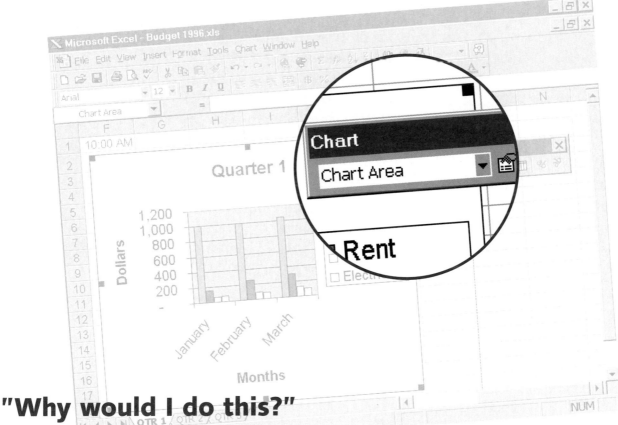

"Why would I do this?"

You can create charts from Excel data using the Chart Wizard. The Chart Wizard leads you step-by-step through the tasks for creating a chart. Excel plots the data and creates the chart wherever you specify on the worksheet.

To create your first chart, continue working with the Budget 1996

worksheet you used in Part 6. If your worksheet still contains a print area (left from Part 6), clear the print area by choosing **File**, **Print Area**, and then **Clear Print Area**. If you don't see gridlines on-screen, choose **Tools, Options.** On the **View** tab, place a check in the **Grid Lines** check box.

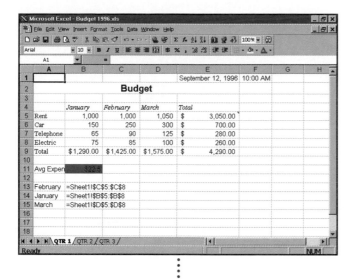

1 Change the data in the worksheet so that your computer screen matches the figure shown here. To redisplay gridlines, choose **Tools, Options**, click the **View** tab, and place a check in the **Gridlines** check box.

Puzzled?

To remove the box surrounding the numbers in one column only, such as Column E, select the numbers in the column, click the **Borders** drop-down arrow on the Formatting tool-bar, and click in the upper-left corner of the box.

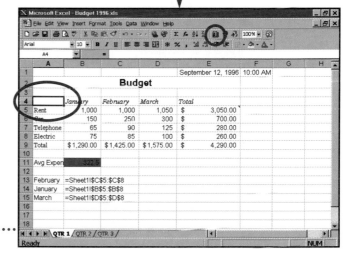

2 Select the cell representing the upper-left corner of the range you want to chart. For example, select cell **A4**. Then click the **Chart Wizard** button on the Standard toolbar. Excel displays the first of four dia-log boxes in the Chart Wizard. From this dialog box, you can preview and choose the type of chart you want to create.

3 Choose a chart type from the list on the left, and then select one of its sub-types. In this case, choose **Column** (the default).

Missing Link

The type of chart you should select depends on what you're trying to emphasize. A column chart tends to emphasize variations over time, while a bar chart tends to emphasize information at a specific point in time.

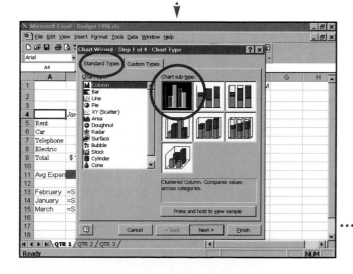

4 To preview the way your data will look if you select a particular chart type and sub-type, select that type and sub-type, and then click and hold the **Press and Hold to View Sample** button.

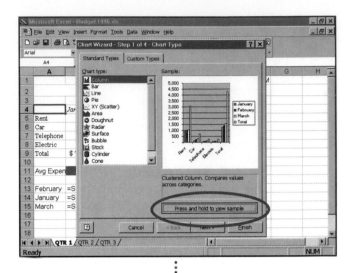

Puzzled?

When you release the mouse button, Excel redisplays chart sub-types.

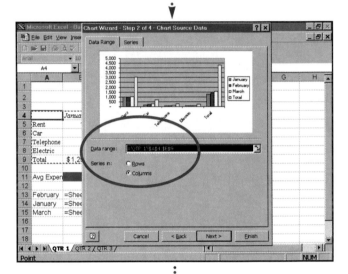

5 Click the **Next** button. Confirm the range you want to chart and whether you want to chart the data series in rows or columns. A marquee surrounds the data Excel has selected to chart—in this case, A4:E9—and the selected range appears in the Data Range text box.

Puzzled?

To stop the Chart Wizard at any time, click **Cancel** and start over. To return to the previous dialog box, click the **Back** button.

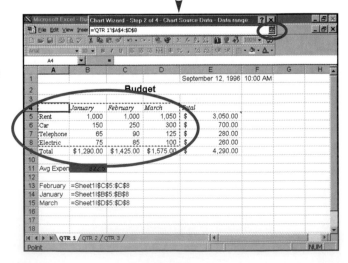

6 You may have noticed, even back in step 4, that Excel is including the Totals columns and rows in the chart. We need to exclude the Total column (E) and the Total row (9) from the charted data. To do so, click the **Collapse Dialog** button at the right edge of the **Data Range** text box and highlight the correct range (A4:D8).

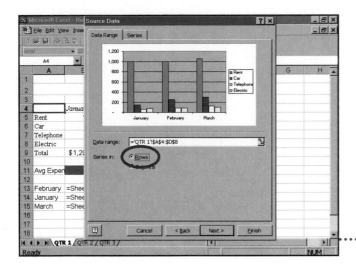

7 Click the **Collapse Dialog** button to redisplay the Chart Wizard. As you can see, each bar represents a month, and you see three bars for each of the four expenses in the budget. Click the **Rows** option button to have Excel chart the data series in rows. In the example chart, each bar now represents an expense in the budget, and you'll see months across the bottom of the chart and four bars for each month in the chart.

8 Click the **Next** button to begin setting chart options. On the Titles tab, supply titles for the Chart, the x-axis, and the y-axis. For the example chart, type **Quarter 1** for the Chart title and press **Tab**. Excel redisplays the chart in the sample box with the title at the top. Add titles for each axis: call the Category (X) axis **Months** and call the Value (Y) axis **Dollars**.

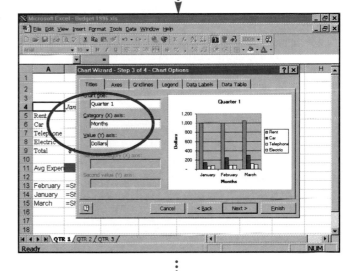

Puzzled?

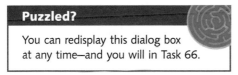

You can redisplay this dialog box at any time—and you will in Task 66.

9 Click **Next**, and Excel displays the last Chart Wizard dialog box, in which you indicate whether to add the chart to the current worksheet or create a separate sheet for the chart. Add to **Sheet1**.

Puzzled?

If you add the chart as a new sheet, Excel adds Chart1 before the current worksheet.

10 Click the **Finish** button. Excel adds the new chart to the worksheet, and the chart is currently selected (as you can tell by the small black squares called selection handles that surround it). You'll also see the Chart toolbar, which you can move by dragging its title bar. While the chart is selected, Excel highlights the charted range.

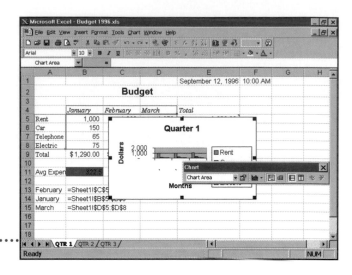

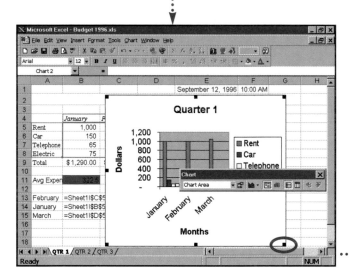

11 You may need to enlarge the chart to see all the data in it. To enlarge the chart, point to the handle in the lower-right corner of the chart. When the mouse pointer becomes a two-headed arrow pointing diagonally, drag down and to the right. You can repeat this action using any handle and dragging in an outward direction.

12 The chart will probably cover some of your data, so you'll want to move the chart. To move the chart, drag it to an empty area of the worksheet. Move and size the chart so that it fits over cells F2:K18. Then save the chart. ■

Puzzled?

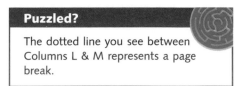

The dotted line you see between Columns L & M represents a page break.

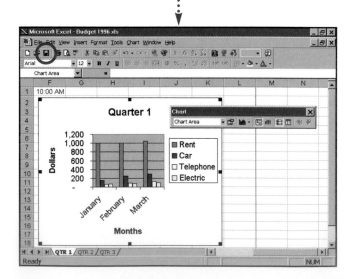

Changing the Chart Type

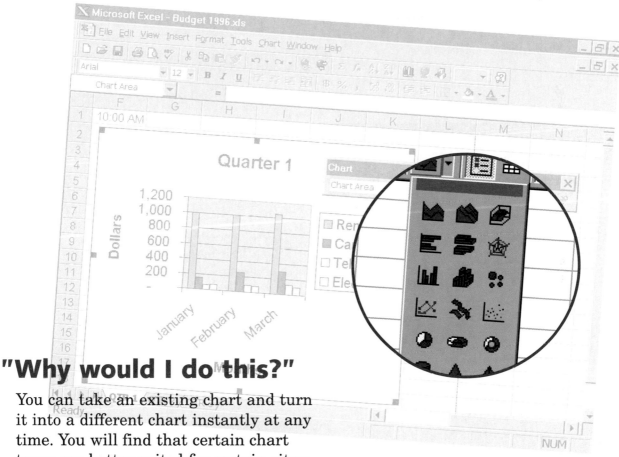

"Why would I do this?"

You can take an existing chart and turn it into a different chart instantly at any time. You will find that certain chart types are better suited for certain situations. It might be more dramatic, appropriate, or meaningful to display the data in a particular type of chart. For example, although you can usually spot trends more easily with a line chart, a pie chart is best for showing parts of a whole. A line chart shows trends over time.

Task 60: Changing the Chart Type

1 If you don't see handles surrounding the chart, select the chart. Point at the outside area of the chart. When the ScreenTip shows **Chart Area**, click. Excel places handles around the chart, and the Chart toolbar appears.

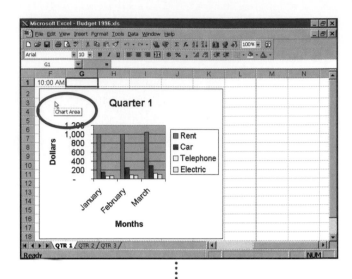

Puzzled?

When the Chart Area is selected, the text in the Chart Objects list box on the Chart toolbar reads Chart Area.

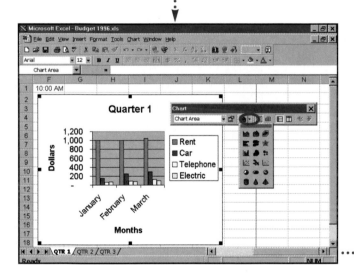

2 Click the **Chart Type** drop-down arrow on the Chart toolbar, and Excel displays the palette of predesigned charts.

3 In the first column, click the second chart from the top. Excel immediately changes the chart to the horizontal column format, showing 3-D horizontal bars. This might look like a good representation for your data, but go ahead and try switching to the line chart.

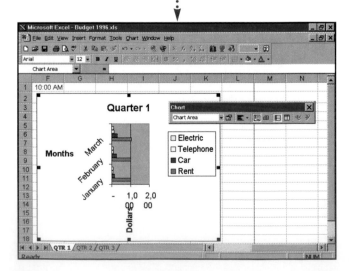

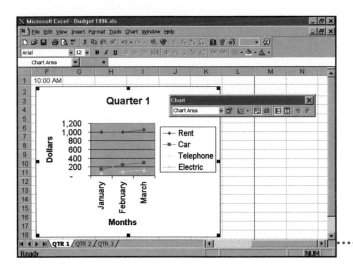

4 Click the **Chart Type** drop-down arrow. In the first column, click the fourth chart from the top to change to a line chart. Excel changes the chart to reflect your choice. Notice that the lines shown here represent expenses budgeted over time. Next, see what the pie chart looks like.

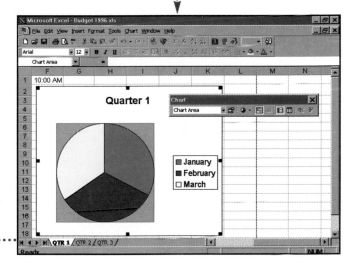

5 Click the **Chart Type** drop-down arrow and select the fifth chart from the top in the first column. Excel changes the chart to a pie chart format, in which each month makes up one-third of the data represented in the chart. Because the pie chart doesn't depict the data as well as the column chart, switch back to the horizontal column chart type.

6 Click the **Chart Type** drop-down arrow. In the first column, click the third chart from the top, and Excel changes the chart to the vertical column format. To best see the chart, press **Esc** to remove the handles from around it. ■

61

Formatting the Title

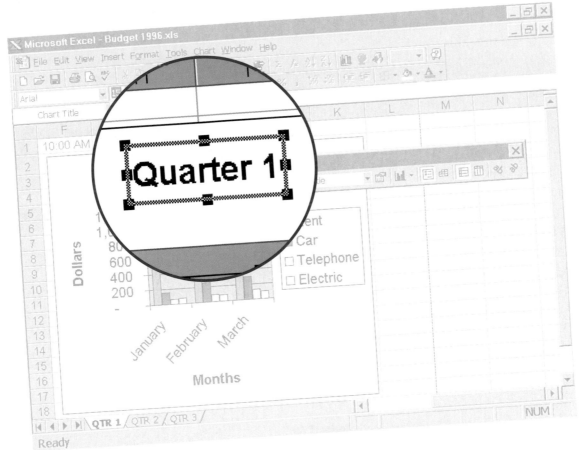

"Why would I do this?"

Excel gives you several formatting
options for the text that appears in a
chart. You can make the text print vertically, horizontally, or stacked. You can
change the font, font size, style, and
color of any text. You can also move
text anywhere you want on the chart.

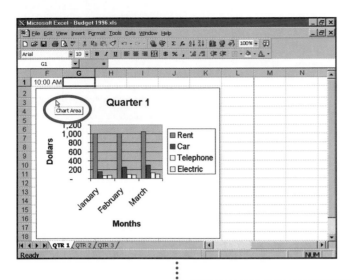

1 Let's make the chart title larger. Point at the outside area of the chart. When the ScreenTip shows **Chart Area**, click. Excel places handles around the chart, and the Chart toolbar appears.

Puzzled?

The text in the Chart Objects list box at the left edge of the Chart toolbar reads Chart Area.

2 Click the title at the top of the chart. A border with selection handles surrounds the title. When the mouse pointer rests on the title, a ScreenTip displays "Chart Title."

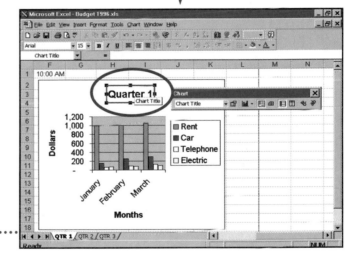

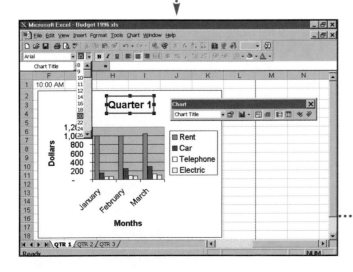

3 Click the **Font Size** drop-down arrow on the Formatting toolbar, and Excel displays a list of font sizes. Click a larger number. For example, click **20**.

Missing Link

The font sizes may vary, depending on the type of printer you have and the fonts installed. You also can type any font size from 1 to 409 in the Font text box.

211

4 Next, change the text of the title. Press **Esc** to cancel the title selection. Then point at the edge of the chart. When the ScreenTip reads **Chart Area**, right-click to display a shortcut menu.

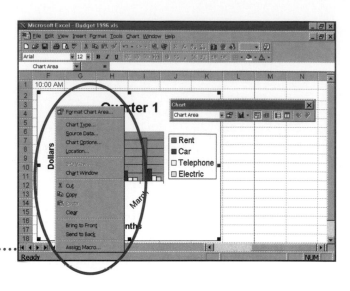

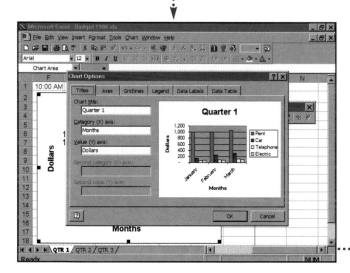

5 Choose **Chart Options**, and Excel redisplays the Chart Options dialog box you saw when you created the chart.

6 On the **Titles** tab, change the Chart Title to **1st Quarter Expenses**. Excel changes the sample in the dialog box. Click **OK**, and Excel changes the chart title. Press **Esc** to cancel the title selection. ■

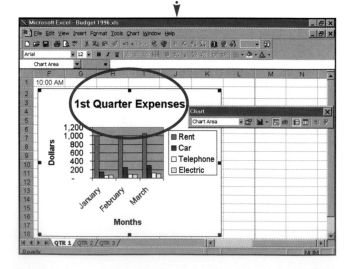

Changing Axis Scales

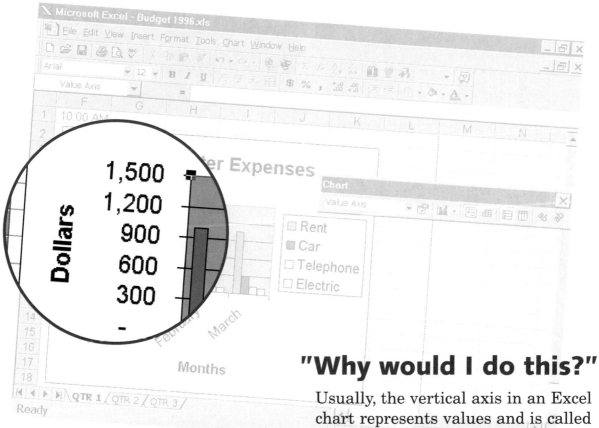

"Why would I do this?"

Usually, the vertical axis in an Excel chart represents values and is called the *value axis*. Excel automatically scales the value axis for your charts to best fit the minimum and maximum values being charted. However, sometimes you might need to customize the values along the vertical or horizontal axis. You might want to display fewer numbers in larger increments on the value axis, for example.

Task 62: Changing Axis Scales

1 Point at the vertical axis (y-axis) line. When the ScreenTip displays **Value Axis**, click to select the value axis. Selection handles appear at each end of the value axis. Click the **Format Axis** tool on the **Chart** toolbar.

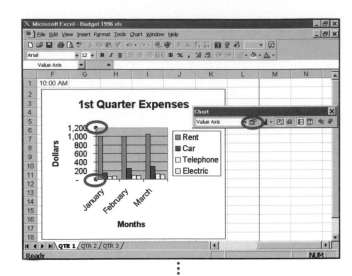

Missing Link

You also can double-click the vertical axis line to display the Format Axis dialog box.

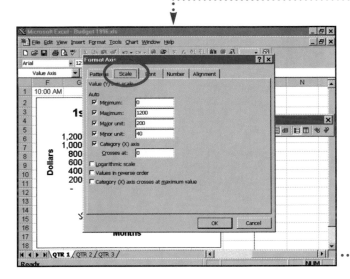

2 Excel displays the Format Axis dialog box. Click the **Scale** tab to display the Scale options.

3 Double-click in the **Maximum** text box and type **1500** to change the high value on the value axis from 1200 to 1500.

Missing Link

When you change any of the preset values, Excel automatically removes the check mark from the Auto check box for that option.

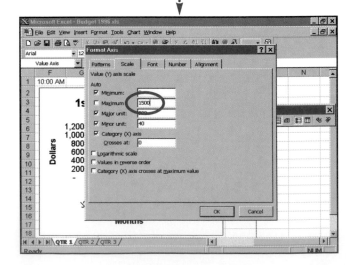

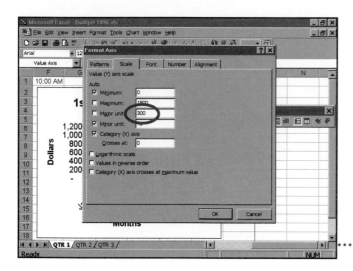

4 Double-click in the **Major Unit** text box and type **300** to change the interval between values on the value axis. Again, Excel clears the Auto check box.

5 Click **OK** to apply your changes. As you can see here, the highest value at the top of the vertical axis is 1500, and the interval between values is 300. ■

Puzzled?

If you don't get the scale numbers you want, click the **Undo** button on the Standard toolbar. If you want to clear the settings and return to the original default values, reopen the Format Axis dialog box and click the appropriate **Auto** check boxes.

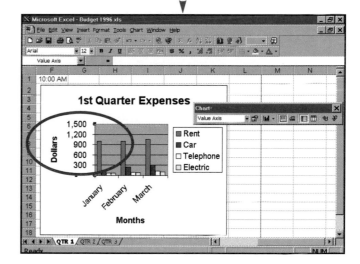

Formatting the Axes

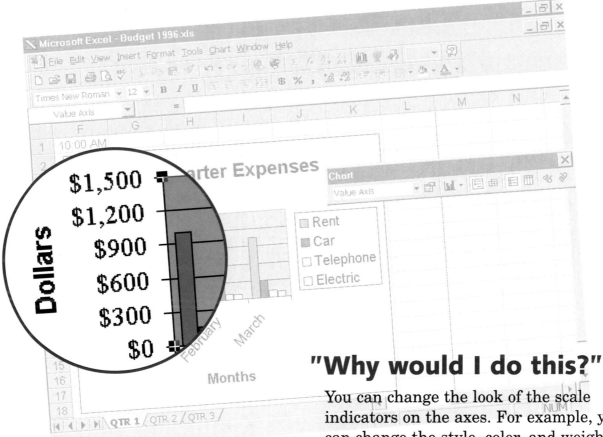

"Why would I do this?"

You can change the look of the scale indicators on the axes. For example, you can change the style, color, and weight of the axis line. In addition, you can change the format of the numbers that appear on an axis scale by adding dollar signs, decimal points, commas, and percent signs.

In this task, you add dollar signs to the values on the vertical axis in your column chart. Then you change the font for the values on the vertical axis.

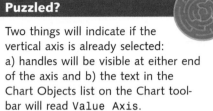

1 If necessary, select the vertical axis. Point at the vertical axis (y-axis) line and click when the ScreenTip displays **Value Axis**. Selection handles appear at each end of the value axis. Click the **Format Axis** tool on the **Chart** toolbar.

Puzzled?

Two things will indicate if the vertical axis is already selected: a) handles will be visible at either end of the axis and b) the text in the Chart Objects list on the Chart toolbar will read Value Axis.

2 Excel displays the Format Axis dialog box. Click the **Number** tab to display the Number options.

Missing Link

You can change the Patterns, Scale, Font, Number, and Alignment options in this dialog box. See your Microsoft Excel documentation for complete information.

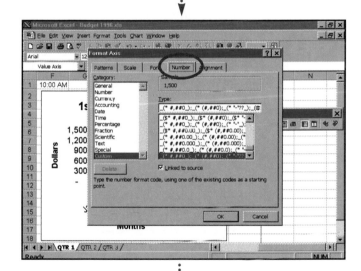

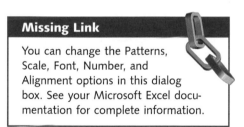

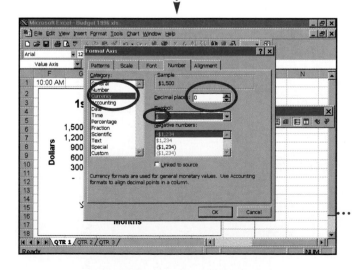

3 In the **Category** list, choose **Currency**. Then open the **Symbol** list box and select **$**. The sample $1,500.00 appears at the top of the dialog box. Use the spinner box to change the **Decimal Places** value to **0**.

217

4 To change the font for the vertical axis, the vertical axis must be selected and the Format Axis dialog box must be open. Because these two conditions are already true (see steps 1 and 2), click the **Font** tab to display the Font options. Then click any font in the list. For example, choose **Times New Roman** to get the font shown in this figure.

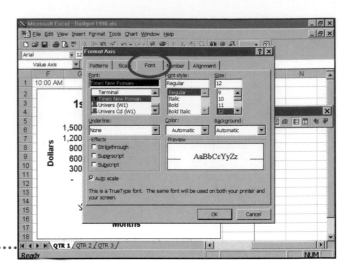

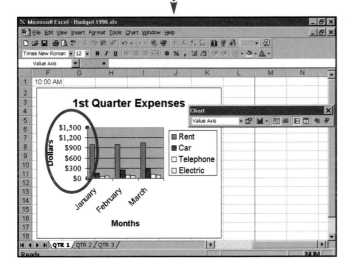

5 Click **OK** to confirm your choices. Excel adds dollar signs to the values on the vertical axis scale and changes the font for the values on the vertical axis scale. ■

Changing the Category Labels

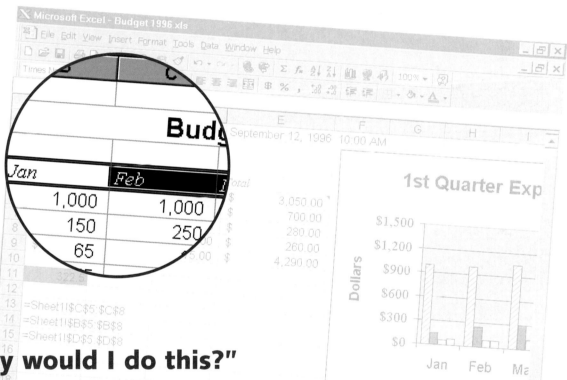

"Why would I do this?"

Excel places category labels next to the horizontal axis along the bottom of the chart. If you don't want the category labels that go with your chart, you can change them. For instance, Excel displays long category labels diagonally. You could enlarge the chart to accommodate the labels, but the chart might look somewhat skewed. Alternatively, you might want to abbreviate long category labels. If you abbreviate them instead,

all the labels will fit properly on the category (X) axis without distorting the shape of the chart.

To complete this task, continue working in the Budget 1996.xls worksheet. If you've just completed the previous task and the chart is still selected, click any cell in the worksheet to remove the handles from the chart and cancel its selection.

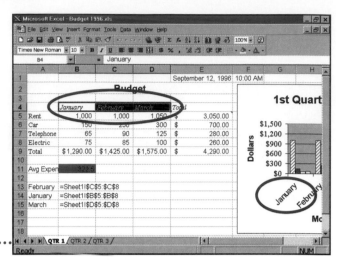

1 Press **Ctrl+Home** to return to cell A1 so you can see the worksheet data. Select cells **B4** to **D4** to indicate the range in which you will enter the category labels for the chart.

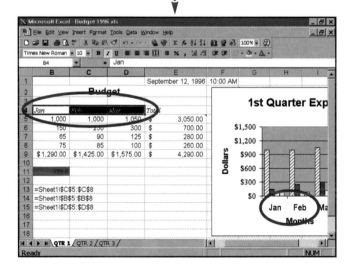

2 Retype the names of the months using standard three-character abbreviations. Press **Enter** after typing **Jan** in cell **B4**. Excel moves automatically to **C4** and waits for you to type **Feb**. When you finish all three labels, scroll to the right so you can see the chart. As you see, Excel instantly updated the chart to reflect the changes in the worksheet. The new category labels appear at the bottom of the chart. ■

Missing Link

The same principal holds true for data. If you change any of the numbers in the cells included in the chart range, Excel automatically updates the chart to reflect the new values.

Adding a Data Table to Your Chart

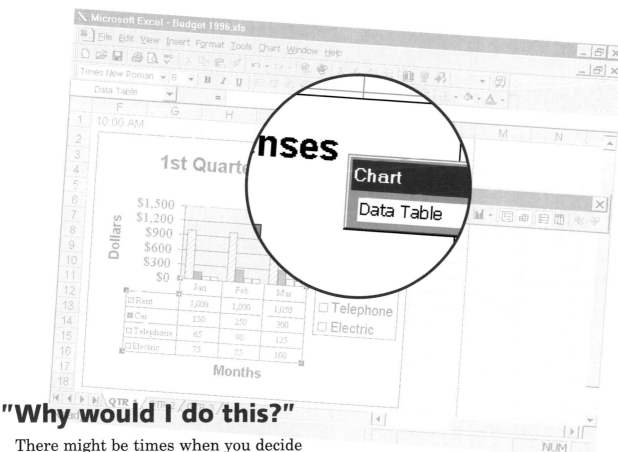

"Why would I do this?"

There might be times when you decide it's most effective to show both your chart and the data it comprises. You can easily add a data table to your chart in Excel using either the Chart toolbar or the Chart Options dialog box. And, just as easily, you can hide the data table.

Task 65: Adding a Data Table to Your Chart

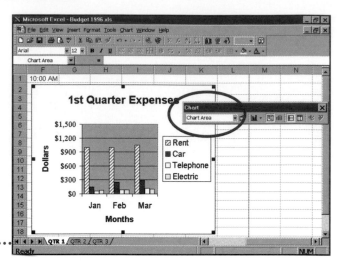

1 If necessary, scroll so that you can see your chart. Select the chart by clicking in the chart area. The Chart toolbar appears, and the Chart Objects list box displays Chart Area.

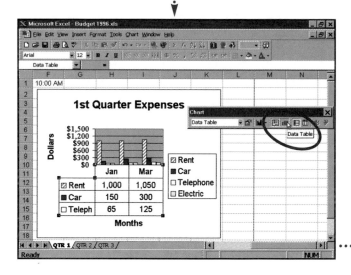

2 Click the **Data Table** button on the Chart toolbar. Excel adds the data for your chart at the bottom of the chart, covering the category axis. You may not be able to see all the data in the table.

3 You cannot change the size of the Data Table, but you can correct the Data Table visual problem in one of two ways: you can enlarge the entire chart, or you can select a smaller font for the Data Table. In this case, change the Data Table font. Select the Data Table, click the **Format Data Table** tool on the Chart toolbar (immediately to the right of the Data Table list box), and then click the **Font** tab.

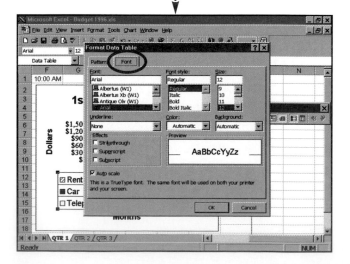

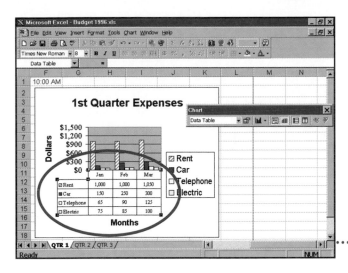

4 Select a smaller font size and, if you want, select an entirely different font. For example, select **Times New Roman 8 point** for the Data Table information and click **OK**. Then click in the worksheet to deselect the chart. As you can see, all the data in the data table is now visible.

5 If you change your mind and don't want to display the Data Table, hide it. Make sure the chart is selected (the Chart Objects list box on the Chart toolbar will read Chart Area). Then right-click and choose **Chart Options** from the shortcut menu to display the Chart Options dialog box.

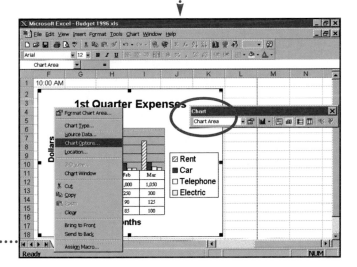

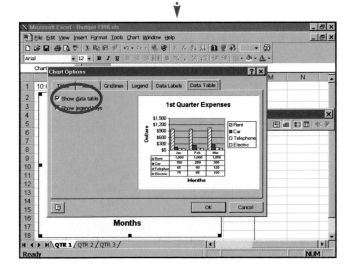

6 In the Chart Options dialog box, click the **Data Table** tab and click to remove the check mark from the **Show Data Table** check box. ■

Missing Link

As a shortcut for hiding the Data Table, you also can click the **Data Table** tool on the Chart toolbar.

Adding Text Labels

"Why would I do this?"

Adding text labels makes the chart's data more meaningful and may accentuate a certain bar, line, or slice of pie in the chart. You might want to add a text label to point out the highest or lowest value in the chart.

In this task, you'll continue to work with the chart from the previous task. You'll create the text label "Lowest Expenses!" and an arrow pointing from the text label to the January data series.

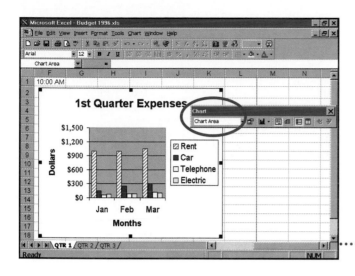

1 Make sure the chart is selected by clicking in the chart area. The Chart toolbar appears, and the Chart Objects list box displays Chart Area.

2 Click the **Drawing** button on the Standard toolbar, and Excel displays the Drawing toolbar.

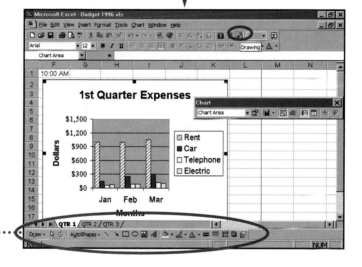

3 Click the **Text Box** button on the Drawing toolbar, and the mouse pointer changes shape. On the chart, below the title, click to create a rectangular text box containing a flashing insertion point (as shown in this figure).

225

4 Enter the text for the label. Type **Lowest Expenses!** and click outside the text box to confirm that you are finished typing text. The label "Lowest Expenses!" appears on the chart.

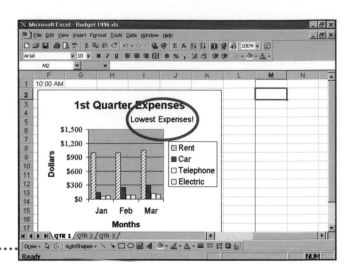

5 Next, modify the font size of the text in the text box to make it smaller. Click the text box to select it. Then select all the text inside the text box and click the **Format Selected Object** button on the Chart toolbar.

Puzzled?

You might find it easier to select the text in the box using the keyboard. Press the **Home** key to move to the beginning of the text in the box. Then press and hold **Shift** and **Ctrl** and press the right arrow twice. Excel selects text one word at a time.

6 Excel displays the Format Text Box dialog box. Select a new font and/or font size, such as **Times New Roman 9 point** and choose **OK**.

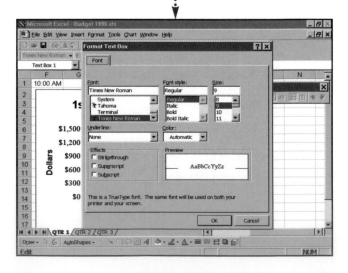

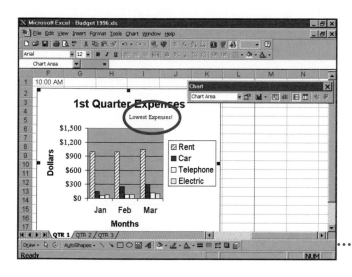

7 Click outside the text box, anywhere in the chart area, to select the chart.

8 Next, draw an arrow connecting your new label to the January information. Click the **Arrow** tool on the **Drawing** toolbar, and then move the mouse into the chart area near the text box. Excel changes the mouse pointer to a crosshair.

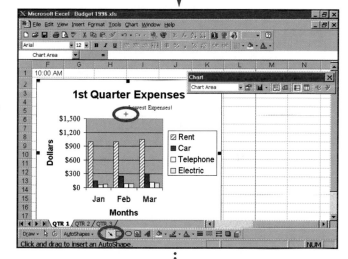

Missing Link

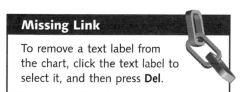

To remove a text label from the chart, click the text label to select it, and then press **Del**.

9 Drag the mouse downward, away from the text box and toward the group of columns comprising January information. When you release the mouse button, Excel displays an arrow, pointing at the group of January expenses. Click anywhere in the worksheet to deselect the arrow you just drew. You can close the Drawing toolbar by clicking the **Drawing** tool on the Standard toolbar. ■

Printing a Chart

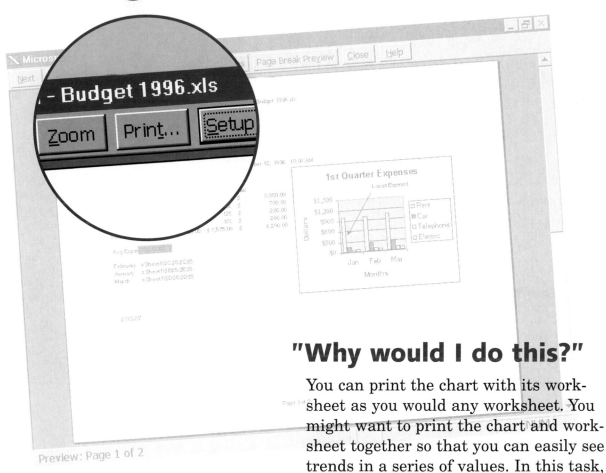

"Why would I do this?"

You can print the chart with its work-sheet as you would any worksheet. You might want to print the chart and work-sheet together so that you can easily see trends in a series of values. In this task, you'll print the worksheet and the chart you created in previous tasks. To print the same information in a different fashion, you can display the Data Table and then print just the chart to print the same information in a different fashion. To print only the chart (which would include the Data Table), select the chart after you perform step 1 of this task.

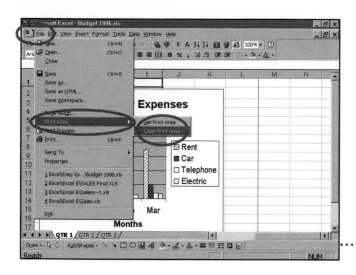

1 Choose **File**, **Print Area**, **Clear Print Area** to remove any previously set print area.

2 Click the **Print Preview** button on the Standard toolbar to display the worksheet on-screen as it will print. As you can see, both the worksheet and the chart appear on-screen in the preview window, but you can see only a portion of the chart.

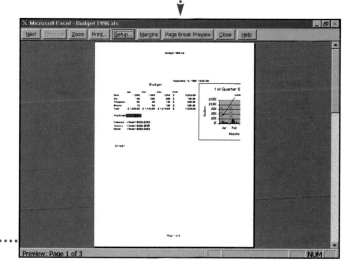

3 To see all of the chart, the best solution is to change the orientation to Landscape. Click the **Setup** button to display the Page Setup dialog box. Then click the **Page** tab if necessary and click the **Landscape** button in the Orientation area.

4 Click **OK**. Excel closes the dialog box and redisplays the worksheet in landscape orientation. Now you can see both the worksheet data and the chart.

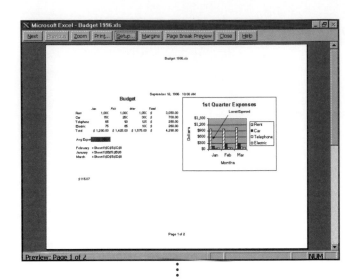

Puzzled?

If you still can't see the entire worksheet and chart, you might want to shrink the information so that everything fits on one page. Click the **Setup** button again and, in the Scaling area of the Page tab, choose **Fit to 1 Page(s) Wide by 1 Tall**.

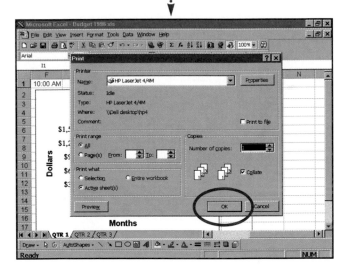

5 Click the **Print** button on the toolbar to display the Print dialog box. Click **OK**, and Excel prints the worksheet and the chart. ■

Missing Link

If you are printing to a printer that doesn't print color, change the print chart options to print in black and white to make sure you get the printout results you want. Select the **File, Page Setup** command, click the **Sheet** tab, and select the **Black and White** option in the Print area.

PART VIII

Communi-cating with Others

▲ ● ■ ▲ ● ■ ▲ ●

WITH THE ELECTRONICS AGE IN FULL SWING, you may find yourself wanting to use Excel for communication activities via e-mail—and you can. Excel links directly to any 32-bit e-mail program compatible with the Messaging Application Programming Interface (MAPI), such as Microsoft Exchange, or to any 16-bit e-mail program compatible with Vendor Independent Messaging (VIM). If you're not sure whether your e-mail program meets either of these standards, contact the vendor of your e-mail program. To use a VIM-compatible program, be sure to install Lotus VIM Mail Support, for which you'll find an option under Office Tools when you run program setup using the Microsoft Office CD. To use a MAPI-compatible program, *don't* install Lotus VIM Mail Support.

From within Excel, you can create a mail message and send a workbook to a coworker. Or, you can route a workbook to a group of people for review, allowing each person to update the workbook and then pass it along.

Using any of the Office 97 products, you can create a *hyperlink* that's similar to those you see on the Internet. But those hyperlinks don't have to be in Web documents. For example, you can create a hyperlink between an Excel workbook and a Word document. Hyperlinks are simply shortcuts you create that open other documents. In Excel, you use the HYPERLINK function to identify the document you want opened when someone clicks the cell containing the link.

Of course, if you prefer, you can create a hyperlink that you use on the Internet—and perhaps place it in a Web page that you create in Excel. You can also create Web forms in Excel, which let users add information to a database through a Web page.

Finally, in the last task in this section, you'll learn how you can easily visit any of Microsoft's Web pages on the Internet from within Excel.

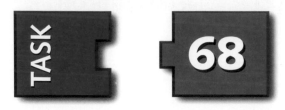

Mailing a Workbook

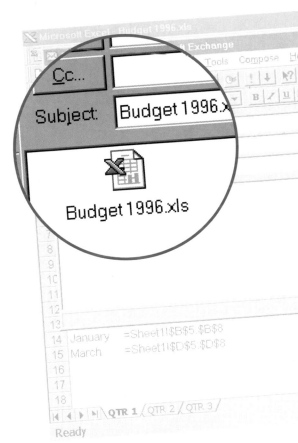

"Why would I do this?"

In the "old days," when you wanted to share a document with a colleague who was not geographically close to you, you could use the United States Postal Service (also referred to as "snail mail"). If you wanted to share a document with a coworker in your office, you could use the network in your office. Or if your office didn't have an electronic network, you could use sneakernet: you get up and run the disk over to your coworker.

Today, however, using Microsoft Exchange, Lotus cc:Mail, or another compatible mail program, you can electronically mail a workbook to a colleague. From within Excel, you attach a workbook to an e-mail message and send the workbook. In this task, you'll use Microsoft Exchange to send a workbook. One word of warning: sending a workbook through e-mail may not work across electronic mail gateways. If you get an error message or if your mail is returned to you, check with your administrator to determine if you're trying to mail across a gateway.

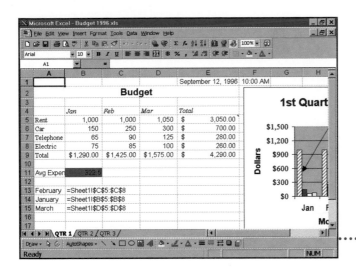

1 Open the workbook you want to mail. For example, open the **Budget 1996** workbook.

2 Open the **File** menu and select **Send To**. From the cascading menu that appears, choose **Mail Recipient**. If you're using a 32-bit mail program such as Microsoft Exchange, you may see the Choose Profile dialog box, from which you choose a mail profile. If you're using a 16-bit mail program and you've installed support for Lotus VIM, you'll see a dialog box that asks you to supply your post office, user name, and password.

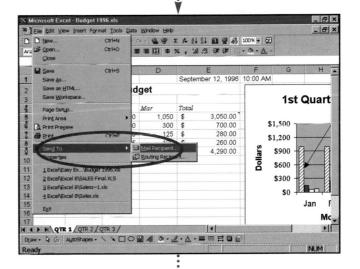

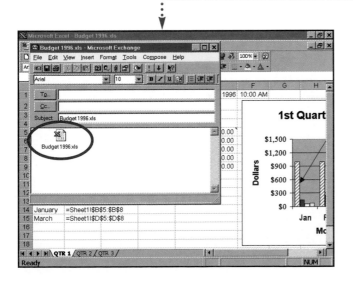

3 The Microsoft Exchange Mail window appears, with an icon for the current workbook already in the body of the mail message. Address the message, add text to the body of the message if necessary, and send the message. ■

Routing a Workbook

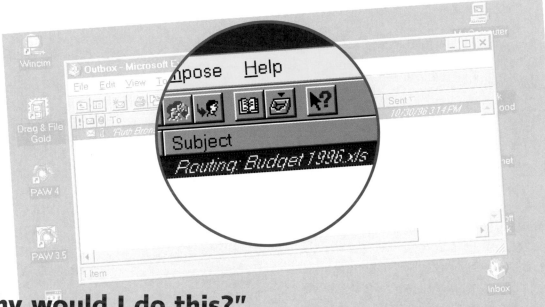

"Why would I do this?"

When you send a workbook (as you did in the previous task), each person on the mailing list receives the workbook simultaneously. However, in some cases, you may want the first person on the list to make changes and send the workbook on to the next person on the list, and so on until the workbook is eventually returned to you. In such cases, you can *route* the workbook instead of mailing it.

When you route a workbook, you can send it to one person after another or to everyone all at once. When the last

person has reviewed the workbook, it is returned to you automatically. To see how this works, create a routing slip and route the Budget 1996 workbook using Microsoft Exchange.

If you are the recipient of a routed workbook, you pass it on by choosing **File**, **Send To**, **Next Routing Recipient**. If you want to send the workbook to someone who isn't on the routing list, choose **Other Routing Recipient** and add the new recipient. To delete a routing slip, route it, and then delete the message from your mail program.

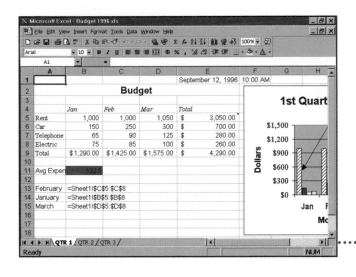

1 Open the workbook you want to mail. For example, open the **Budget 1996** workbook.

2 Open the **File** menu and choose **Send To**. From the cascading menu that appears, choose **Routing Recipient**.

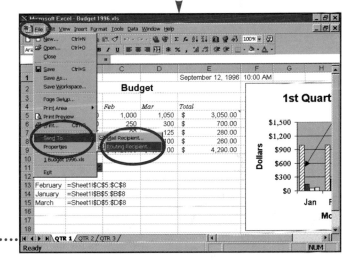

3 You see the Check Names dialog box, asking you to identify who is sending the workbook. Click **Show More Names**.

Puzzled?

You may not see the Check Names dialog box; if you don't, skip steps 3 and 4.

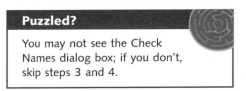

4 Exchange displays the Select Name dialog box. Select your own name (as the sender) and click **OK**.

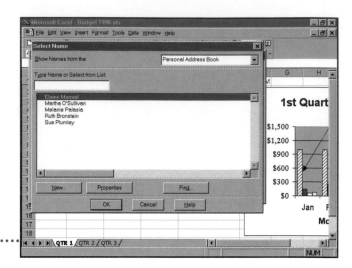

5 You see the Routing Slip dialog box, showing that the message is from you. To add recipients, click the **Address** button to display your Microsoft Exchange Address Book.

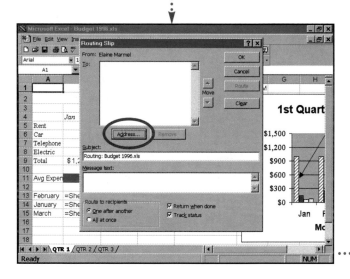

6 Select a recipient from the list on the left, and then click the **To** button. The recipient's name appears in the list on the right. Repeat this process to select everyone to whom you want to send the workbook.

Missing Link

If you intend to send the workbook to recipients in a certain order, save yourself steps by selecting them in order in this dialog box.

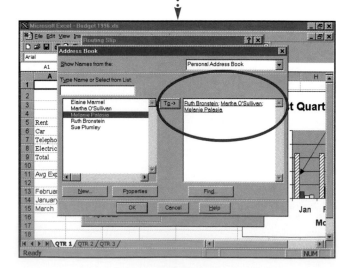

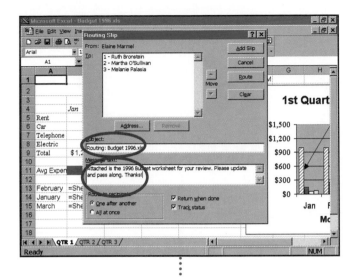

7 Click **OK** to return to the Routing Slip dialog box. If your recipients don't appear in the proper order, highlight a recipient and click the **Move** arrow buttons to change the order. Enter a message in the **Message Text** box to send a text message with the workbook. In the **Route to Recipients** area, choose how you want the recipients to receive the message: in sequential order or all at once.

8 Choose either **Add Slip** or **Route**. Regardless which you choose, Excel redisplays your workbook and creates a routing slip; however, if you choose Route, Exchange also places the message in your mail program's Outbox so it's ready to send when you launch your mail program. For this example, choose **Route**. (Use Add Slip if you're not sure you have included everyone who should be on the mailing list.)

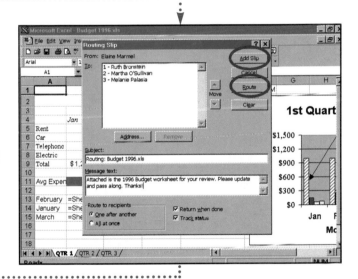

9 Depending on the way your mail program is set up, the message either will be sent as soon as you start your mail program or it will appear in your Outbox, as in this figure. ■

> **Missing Link**
>
> To edit a routing slip, select the **File**, **Send To** command. Choose **Other Routing Recipient** from the workbook's menu, and you'll see the Routing Slip dialog box again. Modify it as necessary.

241

TASK

70

Creating a Hyperlink

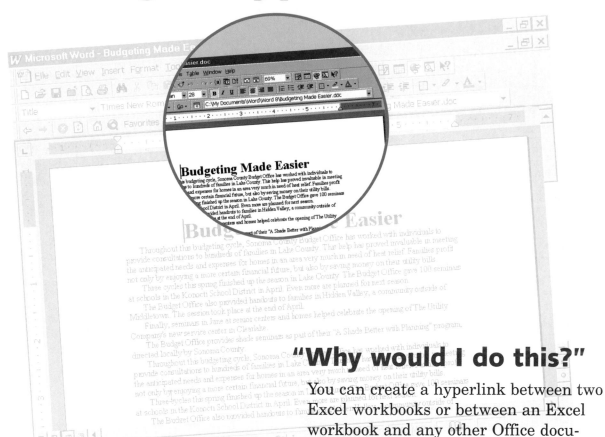

"Why would I do this?"

You can create a hyperlink between two Excel workbooks or between an Excel workbook and any other Office document. A *hyperlink* is a shortcut that opens a document stored on a network server, an intranet, or the Internet. In Excel, you use the HYPERLINK function to identify the document you want opened when someone clicks the cell containing the link. In this task, you create a hyperlink to a Word document.

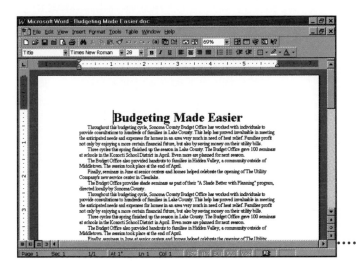

1 If you're going to hyperlink to a document, create and save the document to which you want to link. For example, create a simple Word document and save it. The document doesn't have to be open for you to create the hyperlink.

2 In Excel, select the cell you want to contain the hyperlink. Click cell **B17**.

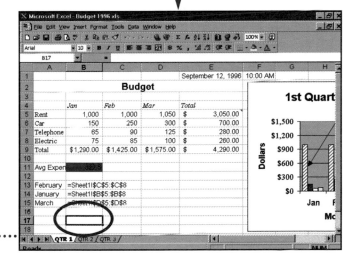

3 Open the **Insert** menu and choose **Hyperlink**. Excel displays the Insert Hyperlink dialog box.

4 In the **Link to File or URL** drop-down list, type the name of the document to which you want to link. (If you're not sure, click the **Browse** button to display the Link to File dialog box, which looks and works just like the Open dialog box. Find and select the file you want and click **OK** to return to the Insert Hyperlink dialog box.)

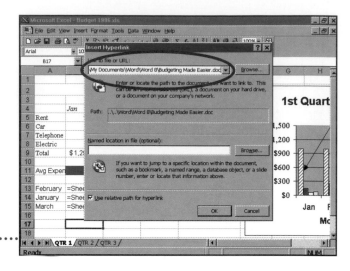

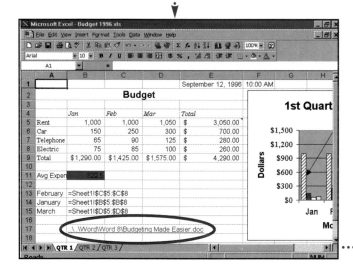

5 Click **OK** in the Insert Hyperlink dialog box, and Excel displays the hyperlink in the selected cell. Move the cell pointer out of the way so you can see the hyperlink.

6 Position the mouse over the cell containing the hyperlink. The pointer changes to the shape of a hand, and the ScreenTip displays the path to the linked document.

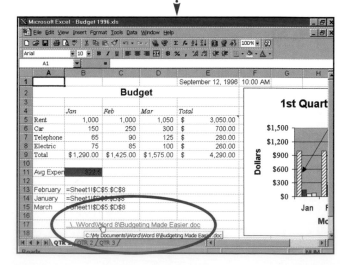

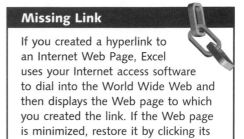

7 Click the cell containing the hyperlink, and Excel displays the Web toolbar and the linked document on-screen.

Missing Link

If you created a hyperlink to an Internet Web Page, Excel uses your Internet access software to dial into the World Wide Web and then displays the Web page to which you created the link. If the Web page is minimized, restore it by clicking its taskbar button.

8 To return to Excel, click the **Back** button on the Web toolbar in the linked document. To redisplay the hyperlinked document, click the **Forward** button. ■

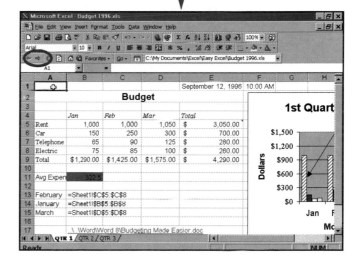

Missing Link

Although the linked document is closed, the program that opened it (in this case, Word) remains open, which makes subsequent jumps much faster. If a hyperlink jump seems to take too long, click the **Stop** tool to cancel it.

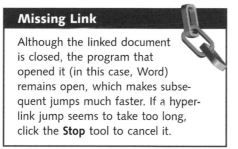

TASK 71

Creating a Web Page

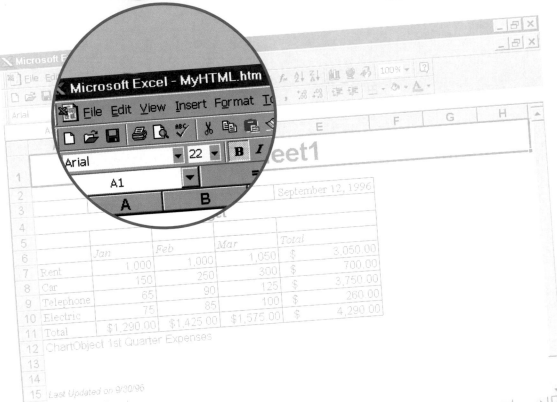

"Why would I do this?"

You can place Excel data, such as numbers from a worksheet or a chart, on a Web page. You use the Internet Assistant to help you.

The Internet Assistant is an add-in program that you must install. If you didn't install it when you installed Excel, rerun the setup program for Excel and be sure to place a check in the **Web Page Authoring** check box located under Excel's available Add-Ins.

1 Open the worksheet you want to convert to a Web page. For example, open the **Budget 1996.xls** worksheet. If you want to place only a portion of the worksheet on a Web page, select that range (such as **A1:E9**).

Puzzled?

HTML stands for "Hyper Text Mark-up Language." It's the language used for Web pages on the Internet.

2 Open the **File** menu and choose **Save As HTML**. Excel displays the first screen of the Internet Assistant Wizard (and the Office Assistant, which is closed in the figure shown here). In this box, remove any ranges and charts you don't want to convert by highlighting them and clicking **Remove**. Similarly, add any ranges you want to convert by clicking **Add** and then highlighting the range you want to add. Use the **Move** arrows to rearrange the order of information on your Web page.

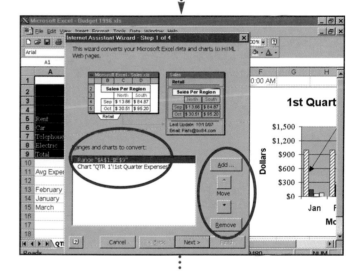

3 Click **Next**. Excel displays the second screen in the Internet Assistant Wizard, in which you decide whether to create a brand new Web page or add the specified information to an existing Web page. Click the first option to create a new Web page.

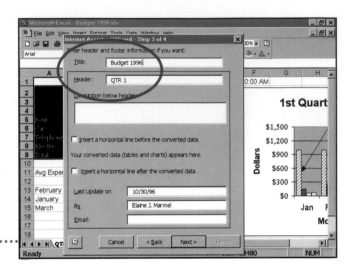

4 Click **Next**, and Excel displays the third screen in the Internet Assistant Wizard. Use this screen to lay out your Web page. Specify such items as your Web page's title and header.

5 Click **Next**. Excel displays the last screen of the Internet Assistant Wizard. Specify the code page, file name, and location for your finished Web page. In most cases, the default code page should work fine.

Missing Link

Save your file as an HTML file and supply a file name with an .HTM extension unless you created a Web site using Microsoft's FrontPage software. Then add the Web page to your FrontPage Web and supply an Internet address.

6 Click **Finish**. Excel closes the Internet Assistant Wizard and redisplays your worksheet. If you open the file you created using the Internet Assistant, you'll see something similar to the figure shown here. ■

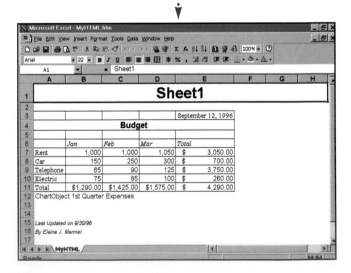

Creating a Data Entry Form for a Web Page

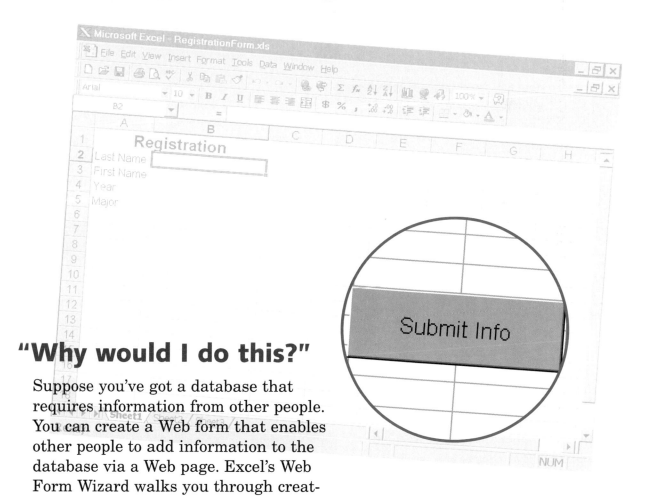

"Why would I do this?"

Suppose you've got a database that requires information from other people. You can create a Web form that enables other people to add information to the database via a Web page. Excel's Web Form Wizard walks you through creating a Web form.

To complete the steps in this task, you must have installed HTML tools when you installed Excel. If you didn't install HTML tools, rerun setup before starting this task.

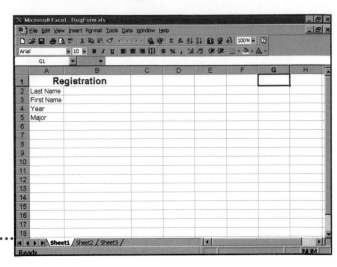

1 Open the workbook containing the information you want to convert into a web form. This figure shows a form called RegForm, with which students can register for classes. To follow along, enter the information you see in the figure.

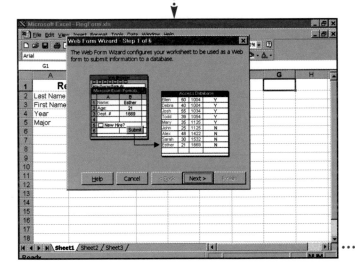

2 Open the **Tools** menu and select the **Wizard** command. From the cascading menu that appears, choose **Web Form**. Excel displays the first of six dialog boxes you'll use to create a Web form.

Puzzled?

The location of the cell pointer doesn't matter when you start the Web Form Wizard.

3 Click **Next**, and Excel displays the second dialog box. In that box, identify the cells and controls you want users to fill in on the Web form. Click the **Add a Cell** button, and Excel switches to the worksheet and displays a collapsed dialog box. Either type the cell address you want to include, or highlight a cell and click **OK**.

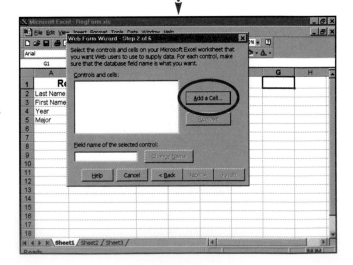

Missing Link

Click only one cell at a time, and click them in the reverse order you would ordinarily expect.

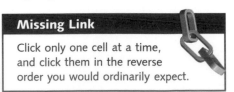

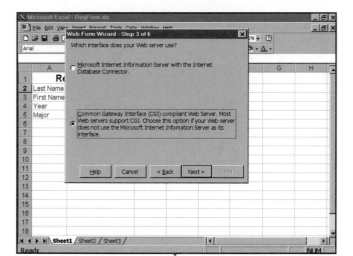

4 Click **Next**. In the third Web Form Wizard dialog box, identify which interface your Web server uses, such as Common Gateway Interface. (See your Web administrator if you need help with this issue).

Puzzled?

Choose Microsoft Internet Information Server with the Internet Database Connector if you intend to store the information users provide on the Web form in an Access database.

5 Click **Next**, and Excel displays the fourth Web Form Wizard dialog box. Choose how and where to save your Web form: as an Excel file or as part of your FrontPage Web.

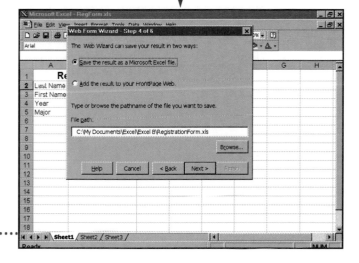

6 Click **Next**. Excel displays the fifth Web Form Wizard dialog box, in which you identify the confirmation message you want to send to Web form users, and where you want to store the information entered by users of your Web form.

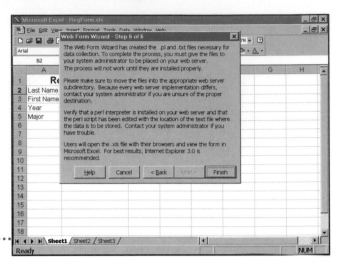

7 Click **Next**. Excel saves your Web form and its related files and displays the last Web Form Wizard dialog box, which explains what the Web Form Wizard has done and what you need to do next to give users access to the form.

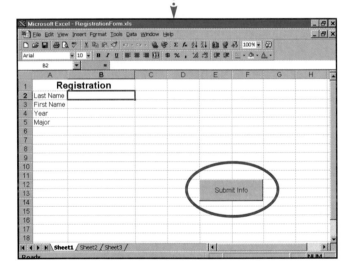

8 Click **Finish**, and Excel closes the Web Form Wizard and redisplays your workbook. If you open the Excel workbook that the Web Form Wizard created, you'll see the form as it will appear to users at your Web site. In this figure, you see the Web form you just created. The Web Form Wizard added the Submit Info button to the workbook. ■

Puzzled?

When you open the Web form workbook, you'll probably see a message from Excel warning you that the workbook contains macros. If you don't know where the macros came from, you should *not* open the workbook until you scan the document for viruses and eliminate any that are found. Because you know where the macros came from in the Web form workbook (the Web Form Wizard), you can safely enable the macros.

Accessing the Internet

"Why would I do this?"

Microsoft has several Web sites that contain lots of cool free stuff (such as templates for Office products), as well as access to technical documents that can help you resolve problems you might be encountering. You can easily access any of Microsoft's Web sites from within Excel if you have a modem connection and access to an Internet account.

1 Open the **Help** menu and choose **Microsoft on the Web** to see the Web pages you can access.

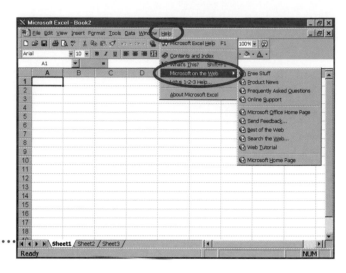

2 Select a choice such as **Microsoft Home Page** from the cascading menu. Excel launches your Internet browser and the software used by your Internet service provider. In the figure shown here, you see Microsoft Internet Explorer (Version 3) and the sign-in screen provided by The Microsoft Network.

3 Connect to the Internet using the method required by your Internet provider. Your Internet access software dials into the Internet. Once you're connected, you see the Web page you selected from Excel's Help menu. This figure shows Microsoft's Home Page: **www.microsoft.com**. ■

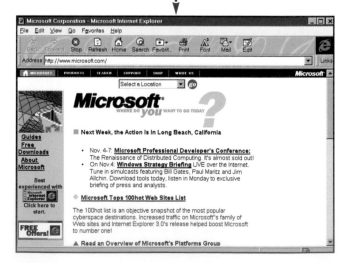

> **Puzzled?**
>
> When you finish working on the Internet, close your browser as you usually would, and Excel reappears.

Reference

Installing and Using the IntelliPoint Mouse

As much as Bill Gates wants people to think that Microsoft is no Cracker Jack operation, the Office 97 packaging is strikingly similar to the Cracker Jack box. If you dig down to the bottom of some Office 97 boxes, you will find a free toy: a Microsoft IntelliPoint mouse (called IntelliMouse for short).

Although similar in shape to the standard two-button Microsoft mouse, this mouse has a small gray wheel between the two buttons. That wheel gives you much more control over scrolling and entering commands.

To install the mouse, follow these steps:

1. Exit all applications.

2. Shut down Windows and turn off your computer.

3. Unplug your old mouse and plug in the new IntelliMouse.

4. Turn everything back on.

5. Insert the floppy disk that came with the mouse into your computer's floppy drive.

6. Click the **Start** button on the Windows taskbar.

7. Highlight **Settings** and, in the cascading menu that appears, choose **Control Panel**.

8. In the Control Panel window, double-click the **Add/Remove Programs** icon. You'll see the Add/Remove Programs Properties dialog box.

9. Click the **Install** button, and the Install Wizard displays a dialog box, telling you to insert the CD or the first installation disk.

10. Click **Next**. Windows searches the installation disk for the installation program. You'll see a dialog box suggesting the installation path, which you'll want to accept. The path shows the drive letter containing the installation program, followed by the title of the installation program. For example, if your floppy drive is A, you'll see an installation path of A:\SETUP.EXE.

11. Click **Finish**, and the installation program begins. During the installation process, you'll see dialog boxes asking for some basic information such as your name. Answer the questions as necessary by clicking the appropriate buttons.

Now you can start using the mouse. The left and right mouse buttons work as they always have, but in applications that support the IntelliMouse (including all of the Office 97 applications), you can do two things with the wheel: spin it and click it. What spinning and clicking do depends on the application you're in. In Excel, you can use the wheel to take the following actions:

- **Scroll up or down a few rows at a time.** Rotate the wheel forward or backward.

- **Pan through a worksheet.** Hold the wheel while moving the mouse in the direction your want to scroll. You'll also notice an origin mark like the one to the left of this bullet. Panning speeds up as you drag away from the origin mark and slows down as you pan toward the origin mark.

> **Puzzled?**
>
> *Panning* is the motion of scrolling continuously.

- **Pan through a worksheet automatically.** Click the wheel and then move the mouse pointer upward (to scroll up) or downward (to scroll down). To turn off automatic panning, click the wheel again.

- **Zoom in or out.** Hold down the **Ctrl** key and rotate the wheel. Rotate forward to zoom in; rotate backward to zoom out. To move to a new location, zoom out, click the cell to which you want to move, and then zoom back in.

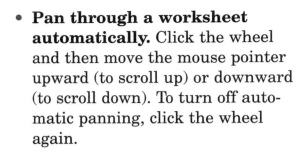

> **Missing Link**
>
> If you find that you zoom more than you scroll, you can set the wheel button to zoom instead of scroll. Choose **Tools**, **Options**, and click the **General** tab. Click to place a check mark in the **Zoom on Roll with IntelliMouse** check box.

To view general Help on how to use the IntelliMouse, open the Windows **Start** menu and highlight **Programs**. Highlight **Microsoft Input Devices**, highlight **Mouse**, and then click **IntelliPoint Online User's Guide**.

> **Missing Link**
>
> You can set the IntelliMouse options the same way you set your old mouse options in Windows 95. Display the **Control Panel** and double-click the **Mouse** icon. The Mouse Properties dialog box displays options that enable you to turn the wheel and wheel button on or off. This dialog box also contains several tabs of options.

Index

Symbols

A

B

C

Index

Index

Index